God's "Eternal Purpose" Now Triumphing

FOR MAN'S GOOD

An Enlightening Survey of the Special
Purpose of Man's Creator, from Its
Formation Six Thousand Years Ago to
Its God-honoring Accomplishment with
Boundless Blessings for All Humanity

To the God who has come to man's rescue
by forming his "eternal purpose"
in connection with his Messiah,
this book is dedicated

CONTENTS

Unless otherwise indicated, all Bible quotations and citations made in this book are taken from the *New World Translation of the Holy Scriptures*, 1971 edition.

In connection with dates, the abbreviation B.C.E. stands for "Before the Common Era," and C.E. stands for "Of the Common Era."

CHAPTER 1

We Are Within the Purpose of a Loving Creator

L IFE on earth is taking on new interest for increasing numbers of people as our twentieth century nears its end.

2 The dying system of things under which we are finding it more and more difficult to live is not the last thing for us to experience. It is not all there is to it for us. Earth will cease to be a place for continual human suffering. The darkening night that now enshrouds all the earth with a deadly pall is about to be dispelled. The new day that must surely follow the night is about to

4

break for all the earth to become a place of joyous living for the whole human family. All of this is not a matter of chance, not a matter of accident, not even a matter of some human scientific breakthrough. Someone higher than man has purposed it.

[3] Yes, increasing numbers of people of all kinds are throbbing with happy excitement as they look forward to life on our same old earth but under a life-giving system of things. Among these the onetime Buddhist who used to fold his hands and pray on bended knee before the gilded image of his meditating god has found new reason for enjoying human life on earth now and forever. The onetime Hindu who used to worship before his triune god Trimurti no longer tries to build up merit for himself under fear of an imagined transmigration of the human soul after death. With a loving interest in all others of mankind he now seeks to share with others the good news that the human family will enter into a better life here on earth. The worshiper who once believed that all his affairs were governed by *Qadar* ("Fate") now wants to prove worthy of inheriting a paradise here on earth, more beautiful even than ancient Damascus.

[4] The onetime Roman Catholic, or Greek Orthodox, or Protestant, who looked forward to becoming an angel in heaven rather than burning forever in a hell of fire and brimstone, now prepares himself for endless life in human perfection on a safe, peaceful earth.

1, 2. Why is life on earth taking on new interest for increasing numbers of people?
3. How have Buddhists, Hindus and believers in Fate been affected by the new outlook on life upon earth?
4. How have religionists of Christendom changed their expectations?

⁵ Marvelous religious transformations all of those! But such transformations are not confined to sincere religious persons. Even the nonreligious have experienced this change of view of life on earth. The onetime evolutionist, who once exerted tremendous faith to believe that human life began accidentally from a tiny, short-lived cell in a primeval sea and evolved ambitiously upward to present human life, no longer depends upon mutations and modern science as to what he will be in the future. The aforetime "godless" Communist, who believed in absolute materialism and who worked for communizing the whole world under an irreligious political government, now hopes for a universal rulership higher than that of selfish, imperfect, dying creatures of blood and flesh.

⁶ All these transformed ones, religious and non-religious, confidently look for life on earth to become better within their own generation. They are now patterning their lives with this assured expectation of grander things to come for earth's inhabitants. Their present lives are happier for this, more useful, more beneficial to themselves and others. Unitedly, they all have this common outlook for the coming years. What has brought about this marvelous transformation in their minds and hearts and lives?

⁷ It is this: They have all come to an accurate knowledge of God's "eternal purpose" and are shaping their lives in harmony with that divine purpose, rejoicing at heart because it is now triumphing for the everlasting good of all mankind. They are humbly grateful that they, too,

5. How have the nonreligious been affected similarly?
6. According to what are all those now patterning their lives?
7. What has brought about this transformation in such ones?

are embraced within the loving purpose of God their Creator. Living within the range of His purpose makes life worth while for them. Eternal happiness is before them.

CHAPTER 2

The Immortal Possessor of the "Eternal Purpose"

"ETERNAL purpose"! Who could have such a purpose but an everliving God? Evolution, as taught by many modern-day scientists, could have no such purpose, inasmuch as accident or chance, with which the unproved theory of evolution begins, does not occur purposely and is without purpose. In the fifteenth century before our Common Era a world-famed lawgiver and poet, namely, Moses the son of Amram, called attention to such a timeless God, saying:

2 "Before the mountains themselves were born, or you proceeded to bring forth as with labor pains the earth and the productive land, even from time indefinite to time indefinite you are God. . . . For a thousand years are in your eyes but as yesterday when it is past, and as a [four-hour-long] watch during the night."—The Bible Book of Psalms, number 90, verses 2-4.

3 In the first century of our Common Era a firm believer in the lawgiver Moses called attention to the same God, who is without time limitations

---

1, 2. Who only could have an "eternal purpose," and what did Moses say about such one?
3. Why could the "King of eternity" carry out such a purpose fully?

in the past and in the future, writing: "Now to the King of eternity, incorruptible, invisible, the only God, be honor and glory forever and ever. Amen." (1 Timothy 1:17) Such an Eternal God can stick to his purpose until it is carried out to success, no matter how long it takes, even ages of time.

⁴ This same writer of our first century C.E. was inspired to write concerning God's "eternal purpose" and to associate it with the long-looked-for Messiah, the "Anointed One" or "Consecrated One," whom the prophet Moses himself foretold. Back there those speaking Syriac in the Middle East called him "M'shi'ḥha"; but the Greek-speaking Jews of Alexandria, Egypt, when making their translation of the inspired Hebrew Scriptures, which has come to be called the Greek *Septuagint,* used the Greek word *Khristós,* which, basically, means "Anointed One."—See Daniel 9:25, *LXX.*

⁵ However, the modern-day translators of the writings of that first-century writer have created a problem for us. From the sixteenth century onward English Bible translations have spoken of it as the "eternal purpose" of God.* But more recently a number of Bible translators interpret the Greek phrase as "a plan of the ages." Thus God is said to have a "plan" in connection with the Messiah.

⁶ For example, the 1897 (C.E.) translation of the letter to the Ephesians, chapter three, verses

---

* See William Tyndale's translation (1525 and 1535 C.E.); the Geneva Bible (1560 and 1562 C.E.); the Bishop's Bible (1568 and 1602).

4. The one who wrote about God's "eternal purpose" associated it with what long-promised one?
5, 6. How have modern translators created a problem as to what it is that God formed in connection with the Messiah?

nine through eleven, by J. B. Rotherham, reads: "And to bring to light what is the administration of the sacred secret which had been hidden away from the ages in God, who did all things create: in order that now unto the principalities and the authorities in the heavenlies might be made known, through means of the assembly, the manifold wisdom of God,—according to a plan of the ages which he made in the anointed." Even as far back as 1865 C.E. *The Emphatic Diaglott,* published by the newspaper editor Benjamin Wilson, contained the reading: "according to a plan of the ages, which he formed." A number of other recent Bible translations could be cited that choose to render the Greek text in this way.*

⁷ Based on this different translation of the Greek text in Ephesians 3:11, there was published in the September, 1881, issue of *Zion's Watch Tower* in Pittsburgh, Pennsylvania, U.S.A., by the editor and publisher Charles Taze Russell, the article entitled "The Plan of the Ages." This gave the explanation of a full-page diagram called "Chart of the Ages." We are pleased to reproduce herewith this chart for examination by all interested persons. A similar "Chart of the Ages Illustrating the Plan of God" was embodied in the book entitled "The Divine Plan of the Ages," published by C. T. Russell in 1886.

⁸ Despite the inaccuracies that are discernible

---

* See Hugh J. Schonfield's *Authentic New Testament* (1955 C.E.), which uses "the plan of the ages." *The Jerusalem Bible* (1966 C.E.) reads: "the plan which he had had from all eternity." The translation by George N. LeFevre (1928 C.E.) reads: "the plan of the ages which he purposed through the Anointed." The word "plan" does not occur in the King James Authorized Version and the American Standard Version of the Bible. In the Roman Catholic *Douay Version* the word "plan" occurs only in Ezekiel 4:1; 43:11 and 2 Maccabees 2:29.

7, 8. What illustration did C. T. Russell publish, and what did his first book say about its title?

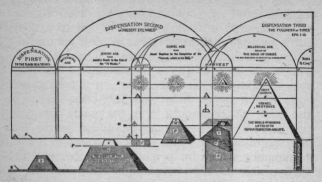

"WRITE DOWN THE VISION AND MAKE IT PLAIN UPON TABLES, THAT EVERY ONE MAY READ IT FLUENTLY."
HABAKKUK 2:2.

CHART OF THE AGES.

ILLUSTRATING THE PLAN OF GOD FOR BRINGING MANY SONS TO GLORY, AND HIS PURPOSE—

"In regard to an administration of the fulness of the appointed times, to reunite all things under one Head, even under the Anointed One; the things in heaven and the things on earth—under Him."—*Eph.* 1:10—*Diaglott.*

in it today, this "Chart of the Ages" served to show the line of sincere reasoning that was based upon the thought that the All-Wise, Almighty God has a "plan." Said the opening words of Chapter I of this book:

The title of this series of Studies—"The Divine Plan of the Ages," suggests a progression in the Divine arrangement, foreknown to our God and orderly. We believe the teachings of Divine revelation can be seen to be both beautiful and harmonious from this standpoint and from no other.

[9] This book attained a circulation of more than six million copies, in a number of languages. Its circulation ceased in the year 1929 C.E. For one thing, it focused the attention of its readers on the Bible and showed that the Living God is progressive. He is getting somewhere with respect to what he has in mind for suffering humankind. We know that a man often forms a plan of action, but that behind such plan of action there is a

9. (a) At least what point did this widely circulated book emphasize? (b) Yet what question did it raise about a plan and God?

purpose to be achieved. But the point in question is, Did the All-Wise, All-Powerful God have to frame a plan of action, a cut-and-dried course, at the time that he made his decision to accomplish something, thus obliging himself as the unchangeable God to stick to this planned course without deviation? Or, was he able to meet all emergencies and contingencies due to free will and choice on the part of his creatures, instantly and without forethought, and still reach his goal? Did he need a plan? Of course, after he has attained his goal, we can check the record of his movements and plot or map out the course that he has pursued. But was it planned just that way?*

A GOD OF PURPOSE

10 Did the original Greek writer of the words in Ephesians 3:11 desire to bring out that God the Creator has a plan in connection with His Messiah? What did he mean when, in his letter written in first-century Greek, he used the word *pro'the·sis?* It literally means a "setting forth or before," thus a putting of something in view. That is why the Alexandrian Jews, when translating the inspired Hebrew Scriptures in Greek, used this Greek word in connection with the holy bread that was placed upon the golden table in the Holy compartment of the sacred tent of worship erected by the prophet Moses. This bread is ordinarily called the *shewbread,* but the Greek *Septuagint Version* speaks of it as the "loaves or cakes of presentation" (*prothesis*). So these loaves, by being set forth upon the golden table,

---

* For the later and present-day position taken on the subject, see paragraphs 14-19 of the leading article entitled "The Son of Man" (Psalm 8:4) and published in the issue of April 1, 1930, of *The Watch Tower* (pages 101, 102). Note especially paragraph 16.

10. What did the Greek word *pro'the·sis* literally mean, and how did the Jews use it in the Greek *Septuagint?*

were put on display, a fresh supply thereof on each weekly sabbath day.—2 Chronicles 4:19.

[11] The word *pro'the·sis* was also used to mean a "statement," or an "advance payment," and, in grammar, it would mean a "preposition." It was also used to mean a "prefixing," or a "placing first." Because the word was also used to mean an end or objective proposed, or a setting before oneself of something to be accomplished or to be achieved, it was used to mean "purpose." (On this, see *A Greek-English Lexicon* by Liddell and Scott, Volume II, pages 1480-1481, reprint of 1948, under *pro'the·sis.*) This latter meaning is recognized by the majority of the modern-language Bible translators. So the "pro'the·sis" of God is his resolve, his primal decision, his purpose.*

[12] In Ephesians 3:11 the word is followed by the expression *tōn ai·o'nōn,* literally meaning "of the ages." So this combination of words is translated by some as "the purpose of the ages"† or "a purpose of the ages"‡ or "age-long purpose"□ or "age-old purpose"△ and by others as "eternal purpose."◊

[13] God's "purpose of the ages" is His "eternal

---

* See *Theological Dictionary of the New Testament,* Volume VIII, edited by Gerhard Friedrich (English translation), pages 165, 166, under "The New Testament."   † *The Book of Books,* by the Lutterworth Press (1938).   ‡ *Young's Literal Translation of the Holy Bible.*   □ *The New English Bible* (1970). △ *The New American Bible* (1970).   ◊ *An American Translation; A New Translation of the Bible,* by James Moffatt (1922); *The Westminster Version of the Sacred Scriptures* (1948); *The Bible in Living English* (1972); *Elberfelder Bibel* (German); *The New Testament in Modern Speech,* by R. F. Weymouth (Eleventh Impression); *The New Testament - A New Translation,* by Ronald Knox (1945); *Revised Standard Version* (1952); *American Standard Version* (1901); *English Revised Version* (1881); *King James Authorized Version* (1611); *New World Translation of the Holy Scriptures* (1971).

---

11. What, then, is the "pro'the·sis" of God?
12. How do modern translators render the Greek expression *pro'the·sis* followed by *tōn ai·o'nōn* ("of the ages")?
13, 14. Why can it be said that God's "purpose of the ages" is his "eternal purpose"?

purpose." How is that? Well, here, an age would mean an indefinite but relatively long period of time in human affairs, with more emphasis on the time-length of the age than upon its phenomena or characteristics.

[14] Thus God's "purpose of the ages" would not mean a "purpose" that has to do with certain designated periods such as a "patriarchal age," a "Jewish age," a "Gospel age," and a "Millennial age." Rather, the emphasis is upon time, on periods of a long time. For age to follow upon age, each individual age must have a beginning and an end. Yet a succession of ages would stretch out the time. And, since in the expression "purpose of the ages" the number of ages is not specified, the number of ages could be endless. So the expression "purpose of the ages" leaves the total amount of time involved indefinite, and it is a "purpose" to time indefinite, with no limit actually marked. In this way the "purpose" becomes a matter of eternity, and it becomes an "eternal purpose." God's purpose in connection with his Messiah or Anointed One had a beginning, but ages of time are allowed to pass before that purpose is realized.* For the "King of eternity" the matter of time is here no problem.

---

* On "katà pro'the·sin ton ai·o'non" in Ephesians 3:11, we read: *"In accordance with the purpose of the world-periods, i.e.,* in conformity with the purpose which God had during the world-periods (from the commencement of the ages up to the execution of the purpose); for already [before founding of a world] it was formed, i. 3, but from the beginning of the world-ages it was hidden in God, ver. 9. . . . *Others,* incorrectly, take it as: the purpose *concerning the different periods of the world,* according to which, namely, God at first chose no people, then chose the Jews, and lastly called Jews and Gentiles to the Messianic kingdom; for it is only the one purpose, accomplished in [Messiah], that is spoken of."—*Critical and Exegetical Hand-Book to the Epistle to the Galatians—Ephesians,* by H. A. W. Meyer, Th.D., English translation, 1884, page 416, paragraph 1.

NOT A NAMELESS PERSON

[15] This King of Eternity is no nameless Person. He has given himself a name and has made his self-designation known to us. What he calls himself bespeaks purpose, his having an objective. How well this fact is brought out on the occasion when God, by means of his angel, encountered Moses, the fugitive from Egypt, at the burning thornbush near the foot of Mount Sinai in Arabia, in the sixteenth century B.C.E.! Moses was instructed to return to Egypt and lead his enslaved people out to freedom. But what if Moses' people should ask for the name of the God who sent him to them as their leader? What should he tell them? Moses wanted to know. His own autobiography tells us: "At this God said to Moses: 'I SHALL PROVE TO BE WHAT I SHALL PROVE TO BE.' And he added: 'This is what you are to say to the sons of Israel, "I SHALL PROVE TO BE has sent me to you." ' "—Exodus 3:14.

[16] God is not here speaking about his existence. A person might think so from the way that some translators render into English the Hebrew expression *eh·yeh' a·sher' eh·yeh'* and *eh·yeh'*. For example, *The Jerusalem Bible* (English translation), of 1966, reads: "And God said to Moses, 'I Am who I Am. This' he added 'is what you must say to the sons of Israel: "I Am has sent me to you." ' " However, God is really talking about being something. This is further borne out by the translation of the *Twenty-Four Books of the Holy Scriptures,* by Rabbi Isaac Leeser, as follows: "And God said unto Moses, I WILL BE THAT I WILL BE: and he said, Thus shalt thou say

---

15. When asked for His name, what did God say to Moses at Sinai?
16. By his answer to Moses, was God referring to merely his existence, or to what?

unto the children of Israel, I WILL BE hath sent me unto you."*

[17] More pointedly, *The Emphasised Bible,* by Joseph B. Rotherham, renders Exodus 3:14 as follows: "And God said unto Moses, I Will Become whatsoever I please. And he said—Thus shalt thou say to the sons of Israel, I Will Beeome hath sent me unto you." The footnote on this verse says, in part: *"Hayah* [the word rendered above 'become'] does not mean 'to be' essentially or ontologically, but phenomenally. . . . What he will be is left unexpressed—He will be with them, helper, strengthener, deliverer." Thus the reference here is not to God's self-existence but, rather, to what he has in mind to become toward others.

[18] Similar to this is when a young person, growing to adulthood, meditates and says to himself: 'What am I going to do with my life? What am I going to make out of myself?' Not otherwise, when the one living and true God was all alone, he had to determine what he would do with his self-existence, what he would make of himself, what he would become. After an eternity of pre-creation existence in his solitariness, he willed to become a Creator. He formed a purpose with regard to himself.

[19] However, the name by which the one living and true God is known throughout the inspired

---

* "Most moderns follow Rashi in rendering *'I will be what I will be'; i.e.* no words can sum up all that He will be to His people, but His everlasting faithfulness and unchanging mercy will more and more manifest themselves in the guidance of Israel. The answer which Moses receives in these words is thus equivalent to, 'I shall save in the way that I shall save.' It is to assure the Israelites of the *fact* of deliverance, but does not disclose the *manner.'*—Footnote on Exodus 3:14, *The Pentateuch and Haftorahs,* by Dr. J. H. Hertz, C. H., Soncino Press, London, 1950 C.E.

17. How does Rotherham render Exodus 3:14 and comment on it?
18. When was it that God first had to decide what to be or become?
19. How did God spell out his name in the Ten Commandments?

Holy Scriptures is not *Eh·yeh'*, or, "I Shall Prove to Be." When, in the year 1513 B.C.E., at Mount Sinai, God miraculously inscribed on stone tablets the Ten Commandments and gave these to the prophet Moses, God himself spelled out his self-chosen name. Writing from right to left, God wrote down the Hebrew letter *Yod,* then a *Heh,* next a *Waw,* and finally another *Heh.* Doubtless God wrote in the ancient style of Hebrew letters, like this: ᚷᚷᚷᚷ; not in the modern-style Hebrew letters: יהוה. The corresponding letters in English, as read from right to left, are HWHY; or, in ancient Latin, HVHJ. All four letters are consonants, with no vowels inserted between these consonants.

[20] Exactly how Jehovah pronounced this divine name to Moses is therefore not known today. For centuries it was spelled by Latin writers as Jehova. Many modern Hebrew scholars prefer to pronounce the name as Yahweh, or even Yehwah. Thus, just as a child does not name its father, so the creature did not name its Creator. The Creator named himself.

[21] This sacred name is in reality understood to be a verb, the indefinite causative form of the Hebrew verb *ha·wah'*. Thus it would mean "He Causes to Become." Now, behind every effect there is a cause; and behind every intelligent cause, or causer, there is a purpose. Naturally, then, the divine name that means "He Causes to Become" embodies purpose in itself. It marks the Bearer of that unique name as the Purposer. Certainly in this capacity he appeared to Moses at the burning bush near Mount Sinai, and what

20. How is God's name pronounced, as based on the four Hebrew letters?
21. (a) Being in reality a verb, what does the name Jehovah mean? (b) Why is it valid to use that name today?

he had set before himself to do he disclosed to Moses. Emphasizing the permanence or enduring quality of the divine name, God said further to Moses: "This is what you are to say to the sons of Israel, 'Jehovah the God of your forefathers, the God of Abraham, the God of Isaac and the God of Jacob, has sent me to you.' This is my name to time indefinite, and this is the memorial of me to generation after generation." (Exodus 3:15) That memorial name has not ceased to be His today. It is a valid name for us to use today.

A MAKER OF HISTORY FOR MAN'S GOOD

[22] In the days of the prophet Moses history was made by the one living and true God, Jehovah, by the way that He dealt with ancient Egypt, the oppressor of the descendants of Abraham, Isaac and Jacob. He made a glorious name for himself by delivering his enslaved people from that heavily militarized world power. (Jeremiah 32:20; 2 Samuel 7:23; Isaiah 63:14) This assures us that the mightily militarized world of this twentieth century C.E. is nothing too formidable for him to take on as an opponent in order to liberate mankind. As he let Pharaoh of ancient Egypt come to power and carry on his death-dealing oppressions of Moses' people, so Jehovah has let the wicked oppressors come to power over all the earth with great oppressions resulting to all the people. There was reason for doing so. It is to reserve them, keep them in custody, for his appointed day to destroy them. So, for the comfort of the heavily burdened people, he inspired wise King Solomon of Jerusalem to say:

22. (a) How did Jehovah make a name for himself in the case of ancient Egypt? (b) What comforting lesson does that furnish us today?

"Roll your works upon Jehovah himself and your plans will be firmly established. Everything Jehovah has made for his purpose [Hebrew: *ma'a·neh'*], yes, even the wicked one for the evil day."—Proverbs 16:3, 4.

²³ Since the year 1914 C.E. it has been an "evil day" for the systems of government that have survived two world wars and associated international troubles. For years now, political superpowers have dominated the earth, suspiciously eyeing one another in their contest for world supremacy. The Sovereign Lord Jehovah, who has created everything for his purpose, should reasonably have a purpose concerning these aspirants for world domination. It is on record that he formed a purpose concerning the "wicked" world powers of ancient Bible times. As assurance of what we may expect for our time, all that he purposed respecting those former world powers he executed.

²⁴ For instance, the Assyrian Empire succeeded ancient Egypt in political, military importance and became the second world power of Bible history. But even in the heyday of its power over mankind, never was it able to boast of capturing or destroying Jerusalem, the capital city of the Kingdom of Judah. Instead, Jerusalem witnessed the destruction of Nineveh, Assyria's capital. Why was this so? Because the Assyrian World Power was wicked. Almighty God, Jehovah, had permitted it to attain to world domination and to act wickedly, especially toward His chosen people. But he had purposed to reserve that wicked world power for an "evil day" at His own chosen time. So about the year 632 before

---

23. What about God's dealings with ancient world powers gives us an assurance of what to expect for our time as to political powers?
24. (a) Though letting Assyria come to world domination, Jehovah was doing what regarding it? (b) Why cannot failure be listed against Jehovah's prophecy in Isaiah 14:24-27?

our Common Era Assyria's capital Nineveh fell to the allied Medes and Chaldeans and was destroyed. (Nahum, chapters 1-3) Thus no failure can be listed against Jehovah's purpose as expressed more than a century beforehand by His prophet Isaiah in the following words:

"Jehovah of armies has sworn, saying: 'Surely just as I have figured, so it must occur; and just as I have counseled, that is what will come true, in order to break the Assyrian in my land and that I may tread him down on my own mountains; and that his yoke may actually depart from upon them and that his very load may depart from upon their shoulder.' This is the counsel that is counseled against all the earth, and this is the hand that is stretched out against all the nations. For Jehovah of armies himself has counseled, and who can break it up? And his hand is the one stretched out, and who can turn it back?"—Isaiah 14:24-27.

²⁵ The Almighty, All-Wise God did not take counsel with anybody in heaven in order to guide Himself in his course of action. "Who as his man of counsel can make him know anything?" is the fitting question that is raised in the prophecy of Isaiah 40:13. (Also, Job 21:22; 36:22; Romans 11:34) His "counsel" is His own, not dependent upon a body of advisory counselors for assistance in right judgment and determination. Hence, his "counsel" here takes on more than the sense of advice; it stands for his express determination, his decree. Regarding the Scriptural use of the word "counsel," M'Clintock and Strong's *Cyclopædia*, Volume II, page 539, says: "Beside the common signification of this word, as denoting the consultations of men, it is used in Scripture for the decrees of God, the orders of his providence."

²⁶ The "counsel" that the Almighty, All-Wise God, of his own self, counsels cannot be broken up either by men or by devils. This was true of His counsel against the Assyrian World Power.

25. In that prophecy, what does "counsel" mean, and why?
26. In letting Babylon succeed Assyria to world domination, what was Jehovah purposely doing?

It also proved to be true of the next succeeding world power, the new Babylonian World Power, the third world power in Bible history. This was the world power that destroyed Jerusalem, for the first time, in the year 607 B.C.E. In doing so, this world power showed itself to be "wicked." So Jehovah reserved it also for an "evil day" at his own decreed time. Before He permitted Babylon to destroy Jerusalem and thereby take on special wickedness before Him, God inspired his prophet Jeremiah to say: "Therefore hear, O men, the counsel of Jehovah that he has formulated against Babylon and his thoughts that he has thought out against the land of the Chaldeans." —Jeremiah 50:1, 45.

²⁷ This prophet Jeremiah lived on under God's protection through the destruction of Jerusalem and its temple by the armies of Babylon in the year 607 B.C.E. But he did not live long enough to see his prophecies against "wicked" Babylon confirmed. However, secular history as well as Bible history record the overthrow of the Babylonian World Power, which occurred in the year 539 B.C.E., in the days of the prophet Daniel. (Daniel, chapter 5) This also confirmed the prophecies of the much earlier prophet, Isaiah, who, not only pointed forward to the downfall of the Babylonian World Power, but also foretold the name of the Persian conqueror whom God would use to accomplish Babylon's downfall. When, in their personal Bible study, the prophets Jeremiah and Daniel took up the recorded prophecy of Isaiah of the eighth century B.C.E., they found written these words of their God, Jehovah:

" 'The One saying of Cyrus, "He is my shepherd, and all that

27. In Bible study, what did Jeremiah and Daniel find written in Isaiah's prophecy about Babylon's downfall?

I delight in he will completely carry out"; even in my saying of Jerusalem, "She will be rebuilt," and of the temple, "You will have your foundation laid."' This is what Jehovah has said to his anointed one, to Cyrus, whose right hand I have taken hold of, to subdue before him nations, so that I may ungird even the hips of kings; to open before him the two-leaved doors, so that even the gates will not be shut: 'Before you I myself shall go, . . . in order that you may know that I am Jehovah, the One calling you by your name, the God of Israel. For the sake of my servant Jacob and of Israel my chosen one, I even proceeded to call you by your name; I proceeded to give you a name of honor, although you did not know me. I am Jehovah, and there is no one else. With the exception of me there is no God. I shall closely gird you, although you have not known me, in order that people may know from the rising of the sun and from its setting that there is none besides me. I am Jehovah, and there is no one else.' "

²⁸ Those marvelous words can today be seen in the Dead Sea Scroll of Isaiah as found in the year 1947 and dating back to the second century B.C.E. The words are found at what is commonly marked in Isaiah as from chapter forty-four, verse twenty-eight, through chapter forty-five, verse six. In the next chapter thereafter, God speaks of Cyrus as "the man to execute my counsel," in the midst of the verses now quoted:

"Remember this, that you people may muster up courage. Lay it to heart, you transgressors. Remember the first things of a long time ago, that I am the Divine One and there is no other God, nor anyone like me; the One telling from the beginning the finale, and from long ago the things that have not been done; the One saying, 'My own counsel will stand, and everything that is my delight I shall do'; the One calling from the sunrising a bird of prey, from a distant land the man to execute my counsel. I have even spoken it; I shall also bring it in. I have formed it, I shall also do it."—Isaiah 46:8-11.

²⁹ The Persian Cyrus the Great did come from the sunrising like a "bird of prey," from Persia to the east of Babylon and from a land that was distant from Isaiah's country, the land of Israel.

³⁰ Quite appropriately, the ensign of Cyrus the Great was a golden eagle, a "bird of prey," and

---

28. In the succeeding chapter of Isaiah, what does Jehovah say regarding Cyrus the Persian?
29, 30. How did Jehovah hold to his purpose as expressed in that prophecy, and in what way does this strengthen us?

Jehovah uses it as a symbol of Cyrus himself. Although expressed in these words almost two centuries in advance, the purpose of the Divine One did not fail. His "counsel" stood, by His use of Cyrus to execute His counsel against wicked Babylon. Jehovah had spoken it, even having it recorded for future reference; and at his due time he did what he had said. He had formed his purpose with respect to Cyrus and had declared it through his prophet, and at his precise time he brought what he had purposed into marvelous reality. These historical accomplishments of the God of prophecy strengthen our confidence in the certainty of all other prophecies in which Jehovah has set forth what he has determined to do according to his own "counsel."

[31] This holds true with reference to a prophecy that history shows has as yet gone unfulfilled, but the time for which fulfillment is evidently getting closer, to occur in our generation. This is a prophecy given through Ezekiel, who was a contemporary of the prophet Jeremiah. It is found in the thirty-eighth and thirty-ninth chapters of Ezekiel. It has to do with the attack to be made by the mysterious "Gog of the land of Magog." This Gog will bring all the nations of this world into this attack. The worldwide attack will be made upon the remnant of worshipers of the one living and true God. Freed from the modern-day Babylon the Great and restored to God's favor, this faithful remnant are living in a spiritual Paradise in the midst of the world's polluted, corrupt condition. What is the reason for the Almighty God to let such an attack be carried out upon His own worshipers? He tells us.

---

31. What prophecy of Ezekiel, as yet unfulfilled, describes an attack—by whom and upon whom?

³² In telling us, God uses in a symbolic way the ancient land of Israel and its inhabitants who were rescued from Babylon to picture the spiritual Paradise of His restored remnant of worshipers of today. Then, in addressing the Wicked Leader of this international attack upon the faithful remnant in their spiritual Paradise, Almighty God made clear his purpose in allowing this vicious attack by saying:

³³ "You will be bound to come up against my people Israel, like clouds to cover the land. In the final part of the days it will occur, and I shall certainly bring you against my land, for the purpose [Hebrew: ma'an] that the nations may know me when I sanctify myself in you before their eyes, O Gog."—Ezekiel 38:15, 16.

³⁴ Nothing could be more plainly stated. The purpose of Jehovah is to sanctify himself before the eyes of all the nations. In accord with all his past performances, He will carry out this unchangeable purpose in the near future, within our generation. After telling how he will use the wondrous means at his disposal to fight a winning battle against Gog and all his international army on earth, the God of unfailing purpose says:

³⁵ "And I shall certainly magnify myself and sanctify myself and make myself known before the eyes of many nations; and they will have to know that I am Jehovah."—Ezekiel 38:23.

WHAT ARE WE GOING TO DO ABOUT IT?

³⁶ Making the worldly nations know who He is

32, 33. For what purpose does God let Gog attack His worshipers in their present-day spiritual paradise?
34, 35. What is God's stated purpose in sanctifying himself in connection with Gog?
36. Why should we ask ourselves whether we want to be drawn along with the nations who are to be made to know who Jehovah is?

will not signify making them his worshipers to be rewarded with everlasting life. To the contrary of this, it will mean the eternal destruction of those God-defying nations! That is a disastrous way of learning to experience who the true God is. He will show the nations just who he is. It has become necessary for Him to do so. Hence, the big question is, Do we personally want to be among those nations that will be drawn into the attack shortly to be made by the Great Adversary of God, namely, "Gog of the land of Magog"?

[37] In all their plans for saving the world situation, the nations are not taking into account the one living and true God, according to His purpose as made plain in his written Word, the Holy Bible. Do their plans sound good to us? Are we going to let ourselves be persuaded by their plans and join in supporting these, thus trusting in human self-salvation? In determining for ourselves what to do, we shall be wise to consider and take to heart what the inspired wise man of old says, in Proverbs 19:20, 21: "Listen to counsel and accept discipline, in order that you may become wise in your future. Many are the plans [Hebrew: *ma-hha·sha·bhoth'*] in the heart of a man, but the counsel of Jehovah is what will stand." Far should it be from our hearts to pit the plans of men and nations against the counsel of Jehovah.

[38] Why should we suffer disappointment with the nations to our never-ending hurt? Let us trust wholeheartedly in Jehovah. "For he himself said, and it came to be; he himself commanded, and it proceeded to stand so. Jehovah himself has broken up the counsel of the nations; he has thwarted

---

37. Rather than be persuaded by man's plans for self-salvation, what course does Proverbs 19:20, 21 counsel?
38. Why will putting confidence in Jehovah not lead to disappointment with men and nations?

the thoughts of the peoples. To time indefinite the very counsel of Jehovah will stand; the thoughts of his heart are to one generation after another generation. Happy is the nation whose God is Jehovah, the people whom he has chosen as his inheritance." (Psalm 33:9-12) Time and again it has proved to be true in the past, and it will prove to be true without fail in the near future, that "There is no wisdom, nor any discernment, nor any counsel in opposition to Jehovah. The horse is something prepared for the day of battle, but salvation belongs to Jehovah."—Proverbs 21:30, 31.

[39] An honest look at the condition of the world of mankind convinces us that we all need salvation. What we as right-minded people want is salvation! This can never come from man himself. We must agree that "salvation belongs to Jehovah." Since "the LORD has made everything for his own ends, even the wicked for the evil day," what must the purpose of the Lord God be for those who are not wicked, those who seek His righteousness? Doubtless a loving purpose! (Proverbs 16:4, *The New American Bible*) Mankind is indeed embraced within the good purpose of a loving Creator.

[40] The Creator is not an aimless God. We his creatures should not be aimless either! At what, then, should we aim? This: To bring our lives into harmony with the good purpose of Jehovah God. There can be nothing higher than this at which to aim. By doing this, we shall really be getting somewhere—toward our enjoyment of everlasting life. In this way our present lives will

---

39. What kind of purpose should God have for those seeking his righteousness, and why?
40. What should be our aim if we want to get somewhere toward everlasting life, and why?

be no failure, for God's purpose will never fail. With this in view, we now take pleasure in examining into God's "eternal purpose" that He formed in connection with his Anointed One, the Messiah.

CHAPTER 3

When Man Was with God in Paradise

HAVE we ever thought about what is implied by the expressions "the Creator of the heavens," also, "God, who created all things"? Those expressions imply that there was a time when God was all alone. (Isaiah 42:5; Ephesians 3:9) No creation existed. So for an eternal past this God was all by himself and he had not yet become a Creator. That is why the prophet Moses said in prayer to God: "Before mountains were born or earth and universe came to the pangs of birth, and from eternity to eternity, you are Deity." (Psalm 90:2, Byington's translation) During all that eternal past before creation God was able to enjoy Himself.

[2] The time came when God purposed to become a Father. This did not mean to become the Creator of lifeless things, unintelligent things. It meant to give existence to living intelligences, to sons with some likeness to him their Father. Thus he purposed to take upon Himself the responsibility of a family of children. What kind of sons did He purpose to produce first? Not

---

1. For how long was God the only One in existence, and why?
2. In course of time God purposed to become what, thereby bringing upon himself what responsibility?

human sons, for in that case he would have had to produce first an earthly globe upon which they could live. Reasonably, God would produce sons who, like Himself, are heavenly, being spirit just as He is spirit. Thus they would be spirit sons, who could see him and have direct access into His presence and with whom he could communicate directly.

[3] The existence of such spirit sons of God is no mere religious imagination. The writer of the Bible book of Job, likely the prophet Moses, speaks of these in the opening chapter of the book, saying: "Now it came to be the day when the sons of the true God entered to take their station before Jehovah." (Job 1:6) A second meeting of those heavenly sons of the true God is called to our notice in Job 2:1. The fact that these spirit sons of God existed in the invisible heavens before the creation of our earth is emphasized when God speaks to the man Job out of the invisible and asks him: "Where did you happen to be when I founded the earth? . . . when the morning stars joyfully cried out together, and all the sons of God began shouting in applause?" Evidently those sons of God, brilliantly shining like morning stars in the heavens, were interested in God's purpose in creating our earth and admired the way in which he created the earth, "stretching out the north over the empty place, hanging the earth upon nothing" in space.—Job 38:4-7; 26:7.

[4] Who was the first spirit son of God whom He created? This one, by reason of his priority,

---

3. How is the existence of the heavenly sons of God, even before creation of our earth, called to our attention?
4. (a) What might God's first created son rightly be called with relation to creation and God's family? (b) How does "wisdom" speak of herself in Proverbs 8:22-31?

would rightly be called the beginning of the creation by God. This one being the first member of God's heavenly family, he could also be called the firstborn of all creation. Our thinking about this here reminds us of what is said in the eighth chapter of the book of Proverbs, where divine wisdom is pictured as a person who talks about himself. Of course, in the original Hebrew text of Proverbs, the word "wisdom" (*hhakh·mah'*) is in the feminine and speaks of itself as a female person. (Proverbs 8:1-4) Of course, divine wisdom does not have any separate existence apart from God. Wisdom always existed in Him and so was not created. For this reason it is interesting to hear how wisdom speaks of herself as a feminine person, especially when she goes on to say:

"The Lord [Hebrew: JHVH, יהוה] created me as the beginning of his way, the first of his works from the commencement. From eternity was I appointed chief, from the beginning, from the earliest times of the earth. When there were yet no depths, was I brought forth; when there were yet no springs laden heavily with water. Before the mountains were yet sunk down, before the hills was I brought forth: while as yet he had not made the land and open fields, nor the chief of the dust of the world. When he prepared the heavens, I was there; when he drew a circle over the face of the deep; when he fastened the skies above; when the springs of the deep became strong; when he assigned to the sea his decree, that the waters should not transgress his order; when he established firmly the foundations of the earth: then was I near him, as a nursling; and I was day by day his delights, playing before him at all times; playing [feminine participle] in the world, his earth; and having my delights with the sons of men."—Proverbs 8:22-31, Rabbi Isaac Leeser's translation, of 1853.

[5] Jewish leaders are concerned about the application that may be made of the above Bible verses. In the Soncino Press edition of Proverbs, of 1945, we read in the footnote on this section: "For the Jewish reader this interpretation is of much importance in view of the Christological use made of this section by the early Church

---

5. Why are Jewish leaders concerned about how those words of Proverbs have been applied in our Common Era?

Fathers."* At any rate, Proverbs 8:22 speaks of something as being created as the beginning of the way of Jehovah God, as "the first of his works from the commencement." A "created" wisdom!

CHERUBS, ANGELS, SERAPHS

6 The Holy Scriptures divide up these heavenly "sons of God" into at least three classes. The first of these classes to be mentioned is that of the "cherubs." Genesis 3:24 describes a number of cherubs as being posted by God at the east of the earthly Paradise to "guard the way to the tree of life." With regard to the nearness of the cherubs to the seat of authority occupied by God and their loyal support of it, the psalmist Asaph speaks, saying: "O you who are sitting upon the cherubs, do beam forth." (Psalm 80:1 and superscription) Psalm 99:1 calls attention to the same thing, saying: "Jehovah himself has become king. Let the peoples be agitated. He is sitting upon the cherubs. Let the earth quiver."

7 Also, King Hezekiah, who represented the Most High God on the visible throne in Jerusalem, associated the cherubs with the heavenly throne of the Sovereign of the universe, when he prayed: "O Jehovah of armies, the God of Israel, sitting upon the cherubs, you alone are the true God of all the kingdoms of the earth. You yourself have made the heavens and the earth." (Isaiah 37:16) Thus, repeatedly, the great Creator, the Universal Sovereign, is shown to throne above

---

* See Tertullian's "Against Praxeas." Therein, in Chapter 7, he says: "The Son likewise acknowledges the Father, speaking in his own person, under the name of Wisdom: 'The LORD formed me as the beginning of his ways.'" See also comments on Proverbs 8:22 by Justin Martyr, Irenaeus, Athenagoras, Theophilus of Antioch, Clement of Alexandria, Cyprian (The Treatises of), Origen's "De Principiis," Dionysius, and Lactantius.

6. What is said about cherubs in Genesis and Psalms?
7. When and how did King Hezekiah associate cherubs with God?

the heavenly "sons of God" known as cherubs.

[8] Besides such cherubic "sons of God," there is a general class of angels. There is no historical reason to doubt the existence of these invisible spirit creatures, for they have made many authenticated appearances to men. About the year 1919 B.C.E. three angelic representatives of Jehovah God materialized in flesh and appeared to the patriarch Abraham as he was sitting under some big trees at Mamre in the Palestinian land of Canaan. Shortly afterward, two of these materialized angels visited Abraham's nephew Lot at the city of Sodom by the Dead Sea, the day before this wicked city was destroyed by fire and sulphur that were propelled through the air upon the city. (Genesis 18:1 through 19:29) More than a century later Abraham's grandson Jacob was returning south to where his grandfather used to camp, and he had the experience related in Genesis 32:1, 2: "And as for Jacob, he got on his way, and the angels of God now met up with him. Immediately Jacob said, when he saw them: 'The camp of God this is!' Hence he called the name of that place Mahanaim [meaning 'Two Camps']."

[9] The Bible word for angel means also "messenger," as in Malachi 3:1, where we read: "Look! I am sending my messenger [or, angel], and he must clear up a way before me." On many occasions the heavenly angels have been sent on missions to deliver a message or with a commission to do a special work. Men cannot block their performing of their commission from God, for they are possessed of power and might supe-

---

8. What in the lives of Abraham, Lot and Jacob authenticate the existence of angels?
9. (a) What does the word "angel" also mean? (b) How are angels used, beyond the power of men to block them?

rior to the power and might of men. The psalmist recognized this fact, and said: "Jehovah himself has firmly established his throne in the very heavens; and over everything his own kingship has held domination. Bless Jehovah, O you angels of his, mighty in power, carrying out his word, by listening to the voice of his word. Bless Jehovah, all you armies of his, you ministers of his, doing his will."—Psalm 103:19-21.

[10] Still another classification of the heavenly "sons of God" is that of the seraphs. These spirit creatures are very reverential toward the person of God. This is borne out by the miraculous vision that was given to the prophet Isaiah. Let us note his description: "In the year that King Uzziah died [778/777 B.C.E.] I, however, got to see Jehovah, sitting on a throne lofty and lifted up, and his skirts were filling the temple. Seraphs were standing above him. Each one had six wings. With two he kept his face covered, and with two he kept his feet covered, and with two he would fly about. And this one called to that one and said: 'Holy, holy, holy is Jehovah of armies. The fullness of all the earth is his glory.'" The prophet Isaiah felt obliged to cry out in a fear of death because of his unclean condition. "At that," Isaiah tells us, "one of the seraphs flew to me, and in his hand there was a glowing coal that he had taken with tongs off the altar. And he proceeded to touch my mouth and to say: 'Look! This has touched your lips, and your error has departed and your sin itself is atoned for.'" (Isaiah 6:1-7) In this we see demonstrated the interest of the seraphs in helping us to be holy as God is holy.

10. (a) What attitude do seraphs have toward God's person? (b) What experience did Isaiah have with seraphs, this demonstrating what?

[11] The number of all these heavenly "sons of God," the cherubs, the seraphs and the angels, runs into the millions. The prophet Daniel in Babylon was inspired to write concerning the vision that he had of a heavenly court scene: "I kept on beholding until there were thrones placed and the Ancient of Days sat down. . . . There were a thousand thousands that kept ministering to him, and ten thousand times ten thousand [= 100,000,000] that kept standing right before him. The Court took its seat, and there were books that were opened." (Daniel 7:9, 10) Such a tremendous number of celestial "sons of God" displays the great creative productivity on the part of the heavenly Father, Jehovah God the Almighty. He has a marvelous family of obedient sons in the heavens. These are not creatures of blood and flesh, for they were created before our earth was created upon which we creatures of blood and flesh now live. So those heavenly "sons of God" are spirit, as God himself is, and they are absolutely distinct in nature from us earthly human creatures.

[12] Showing the sharp distinction between God and men (like the ancient Egyptians) and between spirit and flesh, the prophecy of Isaiah 31:3 discouraged the Israelites from looking to the militarized Egyptians for help, saying: "The Egyptians, though, are earthling men, and not God; and their horses are flesh, and not spirit." Also, in a direct statement that the heavenly "sons of God" are of a nature distinct from that of man, Psalm 104:1-4 says: "Bless Jehovah, O my soul. O Jehovah my God, you have proved

---

11. How large is God's family of heavenly "sons," and why are they distinct in nature from us humans?
12. Why do not the heavenly "sons of God" include now human souls transplanted to the invisible spirit realm?

very great. With dignity and splendor you have clothed yourself, enwrapping yourself with light as with a garment, stretching out the heavens like a tent cloth, the One . . . making his angels spirits, his ministers a devouring fire." Definitely the Sacred Scriptures rule out the religious idea that the heavenly angels include human souls that have been transplanted from earth to the invisible spirit heavens. The spirit "sons of God" were all brothers, all of them being sons of the same heavenly Father.

MAN'S CREATION

¹³ A true father produces a family because he loves children. He has no desire to make fiends or devils out of them or to get any satisfaction out of torturing and tormenting them. He has their highest interests at heart. He wants to find pleasure in them because they reflect his image and are a credit to him and give him due respect and obedience. Long ago, under divine inspiration, a king who was himself a father of many children said: "A wise son is the one that makes a father rejoice." "The father of a righteous one will without fail be joyful; the one becoming father to a wise one will also rejoice in him."—Proverbs 10:1; 23:24.

¹⁴ As regards the attitude of the heavenly Father toward his intelligent creatures, the psalmist David said: "As a father shows mercy to his sons, Jehovah has shown mercy to those fearing him. For he himself well knows the formation of us, remembering that we are dust." (Psalm 103: 13, 14) What Jehovah expects of his sons, he

13. What is the attitude of a true father toward a family that he produces?
14. How is Jehovah compared to a human father in dealing with sons?

indicates, saying: "A son, for his part, honors a father; and a servant, his grand master. So if I am a father, where is the honor to me? And if I am a grand master, where is the fear of me?" (Malachi 1:6) Jehovah the heavenly Father is not inferior to an earthly father in showing the right qualities toward His creatures, for He says: "And I will show compassion upon them, just as a man shows compassion upon his son who is serving him."—Malachi 3:17.

[15] With nothing short of a loving motive, Jehovah God purposed to become father to children of a new nature. This signified that they would not be of the spirit nature, not of the heavenly nature. Theirs would be a nature less refined than that of the spirit nature and hence subjecting them to limitations and restrictions such as the heavenly "sons of God" do not have. However, this would work no hardship for them and would be perfectly enjoyable. Their nature was to be that of flesh and blood, or human nature. The creating of children of this lower nature was not because the heavenly Father had become dissatisfied with his vast family of spirit sons or needed something new and additional with which to provide new entertainment for himself. It was, rather, to display still further the greatly diversified wisdom of God as a Creator, and also to expand his love to still other creatures.

[16] First, however, He must provide the materials with which to create this family of the human nature and also a suitable place for this human family to live and occupy. With this in view, He

---

15. What was God's motive in creating children of a nature lower than that of heavenly sons, and what would thereby be displayed?
16. (a) For creating a family of human nature, what must God first produce? (b) What was his stated purpose for creating our earth?

created the earth, a planet belonging to the solar system that is a part of the great galaxy of stars now known as The Milky Way. At this point the Holy Bible opens up its marvelous story, saying: "In the beginning God created the heavens and the earth." (Genesis 1:1) With loving care he prepared the conditions and environment on the cooled, hardened surface of the earth for its human inhabitants. His purpose for this earth he speaks of, saying:

"This is what Jehovah has said, the Creator of the heavens, He the true God, the Former of the earth and the Maker of it, He the One who firmly established it, who did not create it simply for nothing, who formed it even to be inhabited." —Isaiah 45:18.

[17] His human family would have bodies that needed to breathe in order to sustain life, and so He provided an atmosphere about the earth. They would need water to drink, and so he provided plenty of that. They needed plant life and vegetation as food, and this He provided for them. They needed sunlight for health and for vision, and he removed any cosmic dust cloud that kept the sun's rays from reaching the earth and later clarified the atmosphere to let the sunlight, moonlight and starlight penetrate to the earth's surface. The human family needed regular periods of rest and sleep, and the great Designer of the earth caused it to revolve so that day alternated with night. He caused the waters to swarm with fish and other marine life, flying creatures to take winged flight through the air, and land animals in great variety, all to play their parts in the economy of earthly life. All of this the wise and loving Creator did during the course of six creative periods of time, which he himself called days.—Genesis 1:1-25.

17. How did the Creator foresee the needs of his human family, and how did he provide for such needs?

¹⁸ Toward the end of the sixth creative time period things had been prepared on and about the earth for the heavenly Father to proceed with starting the human family. Then it was that he announced what was to be the climax of his earthly creative work, as we read in Genesis 1:26: "And God went on to say: 'Let us make man in our image, according to our likeness, and let them have in subjection the fish of the sea and the flying creatures of the heavens and the domestic animals and all the earth and every moving animal that is moving upon the earth.'"

¹⁹ In the Hebrew text of this creation account the word for "God" is *e·lo·him'*, which is the plural form of *e·lo'ah*, the plural form being used here in Genesis to denote excellence and grandeur, and not a number of gods, two, three or more. That is why the verbs that here go with *E·lo·him'* are in the singular number. And so when we read, "And God [*E·lo·him'*] went on to say: 'Let us,'" it does not mean that God was talking to himself. He is not a trinity, a triune god, a god in three persons, so that one person of him was saying to the other two persons of him, "Let us." In Genesis 2:4 this Creator is called Jehovah God, and later the writer, the prophet Moses, said: "Listen, O Israel: Jehovah our God is one Jehovah." There are not two or three Jehovahs, only one! A so-called triune god or trinity is a pagan invention. It is a blasphemous falsehood. —Deuteronomy 6:4.

²⁰ Consequently, when God (*E·lo·him'*) said, "Let us," he was speaking to at least someone

18. When and on what creative "day" did God announce his purpose to make the climax of his earthly creation?
19. How can we prove whether God was talking to himself in Genesis 1:26?
20. Most reasonably the words "Let us make man" were addressed to whom, and why so?

else apart from himself in the invisible spirit heavens. It is hardly likely that Jehovah God would be here speaking to the 100,000,000 or more angels who minister to him and asking their cooperation with him in the creation of man. It is most reasonable that he would be speaking to his firstborn heavenly Son, the first-born of all creation, the beginning of the creation by God. This one, as the firstborn of God's heavenly family, would be the one to be given the preeminence and honor of being invited to work together with his heavenly Father in the creation of man on earth. This would simplify matters. Since this firstborn heavenly son bore the "image" of his heavenly Father and was according to His "likeness," God could properly say to him, "Let us make man in our image, according to our likeness." One's being in the image of God and according to his likeness would never mean that one was the equal of Jehovah God. An "image" is not the real thing!

THE FIRST MAN IN PARADISE

21 Genesis, chapter two, goes into detail on man's creation. Descriptively, Genesis 2:7, 8 tells us: "And Jehovah God proceeded to form the man out of dust from the ground and to blow into his nostrils the breath of life, and the man came to be a living soul. Further, Jehovah God planted a garden in Eden, toward the east, and there he put the man whom he had formed." In the ancient Syriac Version of the Bible the word Paradise is used to stand for "garden"; the Douay Version of the Bible also uses the word Paradise and says: "And the Lord God had planted a

21. Where does it say that the newly created man was put in Paradise?

paradise of pleasure from the beginning: wherein he placed man whom he had formed."—Genesis 2:8, *Dy.*

²² Let us note once again what Genesis 2:7 states about the creation of man. Does it say that Jehovah God put in man a soul separate and distinct from his body? That is what many religious people want to read into the text. In fact, the Spanish Bible translation by F. Torres Amat– S. L. Copello, of 1942 C.E., reads, when translated into English: "Then the Lord God formed the man of the slime of the earth, and breathed in his face a breath *or spirit* of life, and the man remained made living with a rational soul."* This is very different from the Roman Catholic *Douay Version,* which says: "And man became a living soul." Also, the version published by The Jewish Publication Society of America reads: "And man became a living soul." In order that our readers may see the literal word-for-word reading (from right to left) of the Hebrew text we present below a photostatic copy of this part of Genesis 2:7 in *The Interlinear Literal Translation of the Hebrew Old Testament,* by G. R. Berry, copyright 1896-1897:

the LORD God formed man *of* the dust of the ground, and breathed into his nostrils the breath of life; and man became a living soul. 8 ¶ And the LORD God planted a garden						
	מִן־הָאֲדָמָה	עָפָר	אֶת־הָאָדָם	אֱלֹהִים	יְהוָה	
	,ground the from	dust	[of out] man (the)	God	Jehovah	
הָאָדָם	וַיְהִי	חַיִּים	נִשְׁמַת	בְּאַפָּיו	וַיִּפַּח	
¹man (the)	²became and	; life	of breath	nostrils his in	breathed and	
בְּעֵדֶן	גַּן	אֱלֹהִים	יְהוָה	וַיִּטַּע	חַיָּה:	לְנֶפֶשׁ
Eden in	garden a	' God	Jehovah	planted And	¹ living	²soul a (for)

---

* In Spanish: "Formó, pues, el Señor Dios al hombre del lodo de la tierra, e inspiróle en el rostro un soplo *o espiritu* de vida, y quedó hecho el hombre viviente con alma racional."

22. What common religious idea do some try to read into what Genesis 2:7 actually says?

²³ Since God's inspired Word plainly says, "Man became a living soul," man *is* a soul. The Bible tells the truth! It is the authority on what the human soul is. The pagan philosophers of ancient time, who did not have God's written Word, are the ones who say that man has inside him an invisible spiritual soul that departs into the spirit realm at the death of the human body. In the Hebrew text the word for "soul" is *neph'esh;* in the Greek Septuagint Version of the Hebrew Scriptures it is *psy·khe'*. Hence, what happens to man's body happens to the human soul. It is not just the human body that dies, but, as Jehovah God says in Ezekiel 18:4: "Look! All the souls— to me they belong. . . . The soul that is sinning— it itself will die." (Also, verse 20)

²⁴ Man is not of the spirit, spiritual. Man is of the earth, earthy: "Jehovah God proceeded to form the man out of dust from the ground." (Genesis 2:7) The body that God created for man was made up of the elements taken from the earth and the atmosphere. It was not a spiritual body, and it cannot be spiritualized so as to become invisible and able to inhabit the spirit realm. It was a physical body, separate and distinct from a spiritual body such as the heavenly "sons of God" possess. Just as a Bible commentator of the first century C.E. said: "If there is a physical body, there is also a spiritual one." The two kinds of bodies must not be confused, and the Bible does not confuse them.—1 Corinthians 15:44.

²⁵ The naked human body that God formed out of dust from the ground there in the Paradise of Pleasure was perfect, none of its necessary

---

23. When the human body dies, what happens to the soul?
24. Why is a "physical body" distinct from a "spiritual one"?
25. What did God breathe into man's nostrils to make him a "living soul," in contrast with Greek philosophy?

parts or members missing. "Perfect is his activity, for all his ways are justice." (Deuteronomy 32:4) "See! This only I have found," said wise King Solomon, "that the true God made mankind upright." (Ecclesiastes 7:29) To make that first human body alive and functioning perfectly, God did not take from heaven a bodyless "soul" (*psykhe'*)* that, according to the pagan Greek idea, was flitting around like a butterfly, and breathe or insert it into the lifeless body. God breathed into the body not a mere current of air to expand the body's lungs. It was nothing like mouth-to-mouth reviving as in the case of a drowned person. What God breathed into the nostrils of the body is called "the breath of life," which not only filled the lungs with air but also imparted to the body the life-force that is sustained by breathing. In this way "the man came to be a living soul."

²⁶ Jehovah God became the Father, the Life-Giver, of this first human soul. Materials for forming the human body were taken from the ground, which, in Hebrew, is called *a·da·mah'*, and so this living soul was appropriately named Adam. (Genesis 5:1, 2) The heavenly Father had a purpose in putting his earthly son in the Paradise of Eden, and He put purpose into the life of Adam. To this effect we read, in Genesis 2:15: "And Jehovah God proceeded to take the man and settle him in the garden of Eden to cultivate it and to take care of it." God assigned to Adam

---

* One of the meanings of the Greek word *psy·khe'* is "butterfly or moth."—See Liddell and Scott's *Greek-English Lexicon*, Volume 2, page 2027, column 2, VI. In Grecian-Roman mythology, Psyche was a beautiful maiden personifying the soul and loved by the god Eros.

26. Why was the first man named Adam, and how did God put real purpose in his life?

his work as that of a Paradise-keeper, a gardener. To give us some idea of what grew in that earthly Paradise, we are told: "Jehovah God planted a garden in Eden, toward the east, . . . Thus Jehovah God made to grow out of the ground [a·da·mah'] every tree desirable to one's sight and good for food and also the tree of life in the middle of the garden and the tree of the knowledge of good and bad." (Genesis 2:8, 9) Containing "every tree desirable to one's sight," the garden of Eden must have been a beautiful place. Among its trees "good for food" was the fig tree.

²⁷ Only a God of love could have given his earthly son the Paradise of Pleasure as his home, the very best that earth had to provide. Being perfect, Adam could have a perfect appreciation of this garden and of its beauty. He was not alone there. There were fish of various kinds in the river that issued out of the garden and that branched out to the regions beyond the boundary of the garden. (Genesis 2:10-14) There was also a varied birdlife, also land animals, domestic and wild. God saw to it that Adam got acquainted with these earthly creatures of a lower nature.

"Now Jehovah God was forming from the ground every wild beast of the field and every flying creature of the heavens, and he began bringing them to the man to see what he would call each one; and whatever the man would call it, each living soul [neph'esh], that was its name. So the man was calling the names of all the domestic animals and of the flying creatures of the heavens and of every wild beast of the field, but for man there was found no helper as a complement of him."—Genesis 2:19, 20.

²⁸ As the wild animals were introduced to Adam, a long-armed hairy creature appeared. Adam named it qoph, which means "ape" to us today. (1 Kings 10:22; 2 Chronicles 9:21) When

27. How did God see to it that Adam was not alone in the Paradise and that he got acquainted with things?
28. On meeting the ape, why did Adam feel no kinship with it?

Adam saw this ape, he did not feel any kinship to it. He did not believe that he was a blood descendant of it. He did not cry out with pleasure: "This is at last bone of my bones and flesh of my flesh." The information that Adam received from God was that *qoph* (the ape) had been created earlier on the sixth creative "day," and that he, Adam, was created separately by God with no flesh connection with the ape or any other of the lower earthly creatures. Adam knew that there are four kinds of flesh. As it was stated nineteen centuries ago, in harmony with the latest findings of science: "Not all flesh is the same flesh, but there is one of mankind, and there is another flesh of cattle, and another flesh of birds, and another of fish." (1 Corinthians 15:39) No, even though God's Word spoke of the *qoph* (ape) as a "living soul," the ape was not found to be a "complement" of Adam and suitable as a companion of him.—Genesis 2:20.

[29] As Adam observed all the wild beasts of the field, there on the ground or on a tree a long scaly animal glided along, without limbs. Adam called it *na·hhash',* which to us means "serpent" or "snake." It did not strike up a conversation with Adam, and he, for his part, did not talk with it. It was a speechless creature, making only a hissing sound. Adam had no fear of it or of other wild animals. He did not worship any of them as sacred, not even the cow. His God had put them in subjection to him, for he was an earthly son of God, made in God's image and according to God's likeness. So he worshiped only his heavenly Father, "the true God," Jehovah.

---

29. Why did Adam not converse with the serpent or worship any animal?

THE POSSIBILITY OF ETERNAL LIFE ON EARTH

[30] How long was Adam meant to live, and where? It was not God's thought that Adam should die and leave the Paradise of Eden neglected. The earth was not to be left uninhabited by humankind. God set before Adam the opportunity for eternal life on earth in the Paradise of Eden. This, however, was dependent upon Adam's eternal obedience to his Creator and God. God put no disobedient leanings, no sinful tendencies, in Adam. God endowed his earthly son with the godlike qualities of justice, wisdom, power and love, with a perfect moral sense. However, in recognition of His own sovereignty over all the universe, it was proper for God, without any suspicions toward Adam, to test this earthly son of His. The test that he put upon Adam was a very small limitation of his freedom. We read:

[31] "And Jehovah God also laid this command upon the man: 'From every tree of the garden you may eat to satisfaction. But as for the tree of the knowledge of good and bad you must not eat from it, for in the day you eat from it you will positively die.'"—Genesis 2:16, 17.

[32] Here the great Life-Giver set before his son Adam the prospect of either eternal life or eternal death. Disobedience to his divine heavenly Father would lead to positive death for Adam for time eternal. Loving obedience as of a son to a father would result in eternal life. The reward for continuous obedience would not mean a transfer of Adam to heaven, for Adam was not made for life in heaven with angels, but was meant for

30, 31. (a) How long was Adam meant to live, and where? (b) What test of obedience did God, not unjustly, place upon Adam?
32. Was eating of the tree of the knowledge of good and bad indispensable in order for Adam to enjoy eternal life?

life eternal in the earthly Paradise of Pleasure.
"As regards the heavens, to Jehovah the heavens
belong, but the earth he has given to the sons
of men." (Psalm 115:16) Adam's eating of the
tree of the knowledge of good and bad was not
indispensable to his living eternally, but "the tree
of life in the middle of the garden" was.—Genesis
3:22.

[33] How, though, was Adam to understand that
expression "in the day you eat from it"? He had
no reason or basis for thinking in terms of a
thousand-year day, according to the much-later
statement of the prophet Moses addressed to Jehovah God: "A thousand years are in your eyes
but as yesterday." (Psalm 90:4 and superscription) He surely did not think: 'Well, if I disobey
and have to die, I may have much or most of the
thousand-year day during which to live; and that
will not be so bad.' Adam had no grounds for
reasoning in such a way. He must have understood God's use of the word "day" to mean a
twenty-four-hour day. Since God evidently spoke
according to the ability of his earthly son to
understand, then, consistently, God must have
meant a twenty-four-hour day. He did not mean,
'In the thousand-year-long day that you eat from
the tree of the knowledge of good and bad you
will die.' Such a meaning would take away from
the forcefulness of God's warning.

[34] Adam got this strong warning direct from
God, even though God may have spoken to Adam
by means of an unseen angel. It was God's word,
God's message. God spoke to Adam out of the
invisible. He did not use some lower animal cre-

33. How, evidently, did God mean the expression "in the day
you eat," and why?
34. How did Adam get the command regarding the forbidden tree,
and how long could Adam have enjoyed communion with God?

ation, like a snake, by which to convey his command to his earthly son Adam. In the latter case, this animal creation could thereafter have been used as a symbol of God and treated as sacred, with due deference. The true God does not want worship rendered to him through an animal creation. Adam in the Paradise of Pleasure worshiped God directly. If he lovingly continued to do so eternally, doubtless such communication with God would continue on eternally. What a privilege it would be for Adam to be thus in the earthly Paradise with God forever!

CHAPTER 4

God Sets Forth His Purpose for Man and Woman

WHEN the first man Adam was alone in the Paradise of Pleasure with only the lower earthly creatures as his companions, God said nothing to him about Adam's becoming father to a human race. But God had this in mind. This was His purpose respecting the earth. In due time he disclosed this divine purpose to man.

² God did not purpose to populate the earth in the same way by which he had populated heaven, by direct creations without use of marriage. God purposed that the man Adam should marry a proper mate, looking to fatherhood. God's thought on the matter was recorded in Genesis 2:18,

---

1. Did God tell Adam, at his creation, that he was to become father to a human race?
2, 3. (a) How did God purpose to produce the human family? (b) Why was no suitable helper to this end found among subhuman creatures?

which informs us: "And Jehovah God went on to say: 'It is not good for the man to continue by himself. I am going to make a helper for him, as a complement of him.' "

[3] God had created all the lower earthly creatures prior to the creation of man and separate from man's creation. Thus subhuman creatures, fish, flying creatures, land animals, were not of man's "kind." They could produce offspring only each "according to its kind." (Genesis 1:21, 22, 25) They could not cooperate with man in producing the human kind. This was plainly to be seen after God introduced the lower earthly creatures to Adam. So the logical conclusion, after man was made acquainted with the animal world, was: "But for man there was found no helper as a complement of him."—Genesis 2:19, 20.

[4] It was still the sixth creative "day," and so God was not violating any sabbath arrangement by continuing to work at further earthly creation. How, then, did he create a helper for Adam as a complement of him? Thousands of years before modern medical science discovered anesthetics and analgesics for performing surgical operations painlessly, God performed a painless operation upon the first man Adam. "Hence Jehovah God had a deep sleep fall upon the man and, while he was sleeping, he took one of his ribs and then closed up the flesh over its place. And Jehovah God proceeded to build the rib that he had taken from the man into a woman and to bring her to the man. Then the man said: 'This is at last bone of my bones and flesh of my flesh. This one will be called Woman [*Ish·shah'*], because from

4. How did God produce Adam's "helper," and what did he call her?

man [ish] this one was taken.'"—Genesis 2: 21-23.

⁵ As Adam had been told how the first woman had been built up from one of his ribs (with blood-building properties in its marrow), he could correctly call her bone of his bones and flesh of his flesh. He had all the more reason to feel that she was a part of him because his own body had contributed toward her creation by God. Precisely right it could be said thousands of years later to the judicial court on the Areopagus at Athens, Greece: "He [God] made out of one man every nation of men, to dwell upon the entire surface of the earth." (Acts 17:26) Thus there is a unity of the flesh throughout the whole human family, such as would not have been the case if God had created the first woman from dust out of the ground in a way separate from the first man Adam.

⁶ After telling of this marriage of the first man and the first woman in Paradise, the divine record proceeds to say: "That is why a man will leave his father and his mother and he must stick to his wife and they must become one flesh." (Genesis 2:24) By reason of the manner of the woman's creation, Adam and his wife were "one flesh" before ever they had sexual union together. The marriage of the offspring of Adam and his wife brings them together in sexual union and in especially this way they become first "one flesh." Leaving father and mother to stick to his wife would mean that the newly married man would set up his own household. In this way the human family would spread.

5. How was a unity of the flesh throughout the whole human family thus attained?
6. According to God's words, how was the human family to spread?

7 There was perfect innocence, pureheartedness, then, in the Paradise of Eden. This is testified to by the statement of Genesis 2:25: "And both of them continued to be naked, the man and his wife, and yet they did not become ashamed." They had a good conscience toward God and toward each other.

8 Here, now, is where the account in Genesis 1:27 ties in, in proper chronological order, now that we have man and woman on the Paradisaic scene. This account reads: "And God proceeded to create the man in his image, in God's image he created him; male and female he created them." Just as before this there had existed male and female among the lower earthly creatures, that these might reproduce their "kind," so at the creation of the woman there existed female and male in the human kind. God is the Creator of sex, but for reproductive purposes. This vital fact was borne out in what God now told the first man and the first woman to do.

9 "Further, God blessed them and God said to them: 'Be fruitful and become many and fill the earth and subdue it, and have in subjection the fish of the sea and the flying creatures of the heavens and every living creature that is moving upon the earth.'"—Genesis 1:28.

10 God blessed the man and the woman at the beginning of their married life in the Paradise of Pleasure. His thoughts and expressions were of the best for them. By his words to them, God revealed what was his purpose for mankind and the earth. God purposed that this earth should be filled with the offspring of this first man and first woman. Not only this, but also that all the earth that this human family would occupy should be subdued. Subdued to what condition? To the condition of the Paradise in which the man and woman found themselves. This meant that the whole earth should be beautified and be made livable by extending the boundaries of the Paradise planted by God till east met west and north met south—to all continents

7. Why were Adam and his wife not ashamed on looking at each other as created?
8, 9. (a) Thus sex was created by whom, and for what purpose? (b) How does what God told Adam and Eve to do bear out this fact?
10. Accordingly, what final state for the surface of the earth did God purpose?

and to all islands of the seas. There was to be no overcrowding of the Paradise earth, but human reproduction was to continue until all the subdued earth was comfortably filled. They were not to kill off the lower earthly creatures, but were to have them in subjection —under loving control.

11 At God's words of blessing and command to them, did Adam and his wife catch the vision of God's grand purpose for them and for their home, the earth? Do we today? Do we today understand the original purpose of God the Creator respecting man and woman and our home, the earth? His purpose is so simply stated, and it is not hard for an honest person to grasp.

12 If we do grasp it, then let us not lose sight of it, for then we shall fall into religious confusion and error. Man's existence on earth was not accidental and was not meant to be aimless. God deliberately put man and woman on earth for a purpose, and this purpose he disclosed to our first human parents. After Adam and his wife, whom he named Eve, were informed and commanded, it was their honorable, blessed privilege to make God's purpose their purpose in life. This would call for their obedience to God. In turn, obedience would result in eternal life in perfect happiness on a Paradise earth, for obedient Adam and Eve and for all their obedient offspring in all quarters of the subdued earth. So life became purposeful for Adam and Eve, and it can become purposeful for us—according to God's unfailing purpose.

13 God set before Adam and Eve no fear of a food shortage as the human family 'became many.' As a loving Father he made ample provision for the earth full of his human sons and daughters. And there was to be no need for killing in the Paradise. God pointed to these facts, for we read: "And God went on to say: 'Here I have given to you all vegetation bearing seed which is on the surface of the whole earth and every tree on which there is the fruit of a tree bearing seed. To you let it serve as food. And to every wild beast of the earth and to every flying creature of the heavens and to everything moving upon the earth in which

11, 12. (a) Why should we not lose sight of God's purpose for man and the earth? (b) How can we make our lives purposeful, with lasting benefit to ourselves?
13. Why was there to be no killing in Paradise, and no fear of food shortage for a filled earth?

there is life as a soul [*neph'esh*] I have given all green vegetation for food.' And it came to be so."—Genesis 1:29, 30.

¹⁴ Here was only a general statement as to what mankind was to eat, a statement that both Adam and Eve heard from God. So it spoke of "every tree on which there is the fruit of a tree bearing seed." It was not here the time to go into particulars, for, in an earlier statement to Adam alone, God had placed a prohibition on eating from the tree of the knowledge of good and bad. (Genesis 2:16, 17) At least for the time being the fruit of this forbidden tree was not to serve as food for Adam and Eve. At any rate, there was plenty of food to eat for sustaining life, without their having to eat also of the tree of the knowledge of good and bad. Even with all the abundance of every food in the Paradise, it was true of Adam and Eve the same as it was true of Jehovah's chosen people more than two thousand years later: "Not by bread alone does man live but by every expression of Jehovah's mouth does man live." (Deuteronomy 8:3) If Adam and Eve kept the word of command expressed by Jehovah God, they would live forever with their family in the earth-wide Paradise.

END OF THE SIXTH CREATIVE "DAY"

¹⁵ Thus at God's marked time the affairs of earth were brought to this stage as described, with marvelous possibilities ahead according to God's purpose. As we view the situation, with the earth now inhabited by human and animal creatures and revolving around the sun and with the moon in orbit around the earth, how does it look to us? Our view ought not to differ from that of God, concerning which we read: "After that God saw everything he had made and, look! it was very good. And there came to be evening and there came to be morning, a sixth day."—Genesis 1:31.

¹⁶ Jehovah, as a progressive God, had been proceeding in an orderly way, in stages. And what logical progres-

14. (a) Besides that general statement by God on food, what prohibition on eating food still applied? (b) Adam and Eve needed to live by what, in addition to material food?
15. At the end of the sixth creative "day," how did earthly creation look to God?
16. What must have been the reaction of the "morning stars" and the "sons of God" on viewing the earth at the end of the sixth "day"?

sion on His part there was! With the creation of Adam and Eve and the divine blessing upon them there came to an end the sixth creative "day" of God with regard to preparing the earth for occupation by earthly children of God. If, at the mere founding of the earth, "the morning stars joyfully cried out together, and all the sons of God began shouting in applause," what expressions of admiration and praise these heavenly "sons of God" must have made at the close of the sixth creative "day" when they saw the earth now in a fully prepared state and a perfect human pair living upon it!—Job 38:7; Genesis 1:28.

[17] The "morning" of that sixth creative "day" ended with glorious divine accomplishment. Would the cycle of creative "days" end with the sixth? The sixth "day" ended with just the foundation laid in Adam and Eve for the populating of the whole earth. Would there be another creative "day," a seventh "day," at the close of the "morning" of which the whole earth would be populated with a human family and be a global Paradise?

"EVENING" OF SEVENTH CREATIVE "DAY" BEGINS, 4026 B.C.E.

[18] God's purpose with reference to the earth was not fully accomplished by the end of the sixth creative "day." The question remained, Could God accomplish this purpose, especially now that he was dealing with human creatures who had the power of personal will and whom he left free to choose their earthly course, either in line with God's purpose or against it? Reasonably, then, another creative "day," a seventh "day," should be allowed for, during which to have the earth populated with a perfect human race, all of them dwelling together in love and peace and all speaking the same language in a global Paradise. The end of such a creative "day" could witness the purpose of God triumphantly accomplished, in vindication of Him as Creator and Universal Sovereign.

[19] God did make known the fullness of his purpose.

17. In view of the divine accomplishment by the end of the "morning" of the sixth "day," what question arises about the number of creative "days"?
18. Reasonably, with what end in view should another creative "day" be allowed for?
19. (a) Why should the seventh one be called a "creative" day? (b) What did God do with regard to that "seventh day"?

It did call for a seventh creative "day." Our calling it a "creative" day does not mean that God kept on creating earthly things on the seventh creative "day," but that it was inseparably connected up with the previous six creative "days" and it was of the same time length as those previous "days." What does God's own Word say about it?

"Thus the heavens and the earth and all their army came to their completion. And by the seventh day God came to the completion of his work that he had made, and he proceeded to rest on the seventh day from all his work that he had made. And God proceeded to bless the seventh day and make it sacred, because on it he has been resting from all his work that God has created for the purpose of making."—Genesis 2:1-3.

20 Let us not overlook the fact that this account of the seventh creative "day" does not conclude with the words that definitely say that the particular creative "day" of an evening and a morning ended. Genesis 2:3 does not add the words: "And there came to be evening and there came to be morning, a seventh day." The failure of such terminal words to appear indicates that the seventh creative "day" had not yet ended by the time that the prophet Moses finished writing the Pentateuch or first "five books" of the Bible, in the year 2553 *Anno Mundi* or 1473 B.C.E. Still later the psalmist David speaks of entering into God's rest, in Psalm 95:7-11, or by the year 2989 A.M. or 1037 B.C.E. This indicates that Genesis 2:1-3, in speaking about God's rest day, was not speaking of a twenty-four-hour day, but was speaking of a creative "day" of the same length as each of the preceding creative "days." So that creative "seventh day" has not ended even as yet.

21 Accordingly, not yet do we see the Edenic Paradise extended all around our earthly globe and everywhere inhabited by a perfect, undying human family. Instead, animal life, birdlife and fish life are being killed off, and the superpowers of the world, equipped with nuclear bombs and other weapons of mass destruction, threaten to kill off all mankind and leave the earthly globe an uninhabited waste. Certainly mankind as a whole, yes, even those religious bodies that claim to

20. How do we determine whether Genesis 2:1-3 was speaking of a twenty-four-hour day or of a creative period that still continues?
21. What situation on the earth indicates that mankind as a whole has not entered into the sabbath-keeping of God's "seventh day"?

worship the God of the Holy Bible, have not entered into God's rest, keeping his creative "seventh day." And now it is almost six thousand years since man's creation!

22 That the account in Genesis 2:1-3 is not speaking of the "seventh day" as a twenty-four-hour day is plain from the use of the word "day" in the very next verse. There, in Genesis 2:4, it is written: "This is a history of the heavens and the earth in the TIME of their being created, in the DAY that Jehovah God made earth and heaven." That "day" included six creative "days," as described in Genesis, chapter one.

23 From the state of affairs of mankind in this twentieth century C.E., nothing could be plainer than that the realization of God's purpose by the end of the seventh creative "day" lies yet ahead of us. At the beginning of this "seventh day" almost six thousand years ago God "proceeded to bless the seventh day and make it sacred." According to the history of mankind during the past six millenniums, it has not been a blessed day for the whole human race. Apparently, the blessing of God upon this seventh "day" has counted for little in behalf of all mankind.

24 Although God sanctified it or made it sacred, very few of mankind are holding it as sacred, holy, and have entered into God's rest in a spiritual way. God will certainly have to show by the end of the seventh creative "day" that his blessing upon the day has had real value for mankind. He will have to show that this "seventh day" has had real sacredness, holiness, sanctity, and that his "rest" as regards the sureness about the accomplishment of his purpose has not been disturbed. Despite his desisting from works of earthly creation at the end of the sixth creative "day," his purpose has marched forward and still marches forward to its triumphant realization. Hence, there is no need for discouragement on the part of those who, like Jehovah God himself, have faith in the ultimate working out of his magnificent purpose.

22. How does the next verse (Genesis 2:4) prove that God is not talking of a twenty-four-hour day?
23, 24. (a) What shows that the realization of God's purpose by the end of his "seventh day" lies yet ahead? (b) Why is there no need for discouragement on our part for putting faith in God's working out his magnificent purpose?

CHAPTER 5

God's "Eternal Purpose" in His Anointed One Is Formed

HUMAN life on earth can be beautiful. The life of man's Creator is beautiful. It is His will that the life of His human creation should also be beautiful. It is mankind that has made a wreck of its existence. Not all members of mankind have done so, however. In spite of mankind's failure till now, the Creator's benevolent purpose now is that men and women will yet have the opportunity to make life on earth beautiful for themselves.

2 At the start mankind's life was beautiful. It started off nearly six thousand years ago in an earthly Paradise. It was a pleasure to live there, which is why it was called the Garden of Eden, or Paradise of Pleasure. (Genesis 2:8, Douay Version Bible) Our first human parents, the first man and the first woman, were perfect, abounding in health and with the prospect of never dying. Being human, they were mortal, but before them lay the opportunity offered by their Creator of living in the Paradise of Pleasure for all time to come, eternally. Thus their heavenly Life-Giver could become their Eternal Father. He did not plan for them to die by taking the course that would lead to death. His desire was for them to live eternally as his everlasting children. More than three thousand years later He expressed his sincere feelings on the matter, when he said to his chosen people:

"'Do I take any delight at all in the death of someone wicked,' is the utterance of the Sovereign Lord Jehovah, 'and not in that he should turn back from his ways and actually keep living?'"—Ezekiel 18:23.

1. What kind of life on earth is it God's purpose for mankind to have?
2. (a) With what kind of living did mankind start off? (b) What shows whether God *planned* for man to take the course leading to death?

54

[3] So the Creator had no desire that the innocent human couple in the Paradise of Pleasure should turn "wicked" and deserve to die. His desire was for them to keep living, yes, living on to see the whole earth properly filled with offspring just as perfect and happy as themselves, in peaceful, loving relationship with their Creator, their heavenly Father. Yet, today, all mankind are dying off, and our polluted earth is far from being a paradise. Why is this? Man's Creator has had the explanation recorded in the Bible.

[4] The location is the Paradise of Pleasure, as chapter three of the Bible book of Genesis opens up. All lower forms of earthly creatures are in subjection to our first human parents, Adam and Eve. They do not fear any of these lower earthly creatures, not even snakes. Yes, there were snakes or serpents in the Paradise of Pleasure, and they were interesting to watch. Their limbless way of locomotion was marvelous, a manifestation of God's diversified wisdom in designing. They are shy creatures, however. Genesis 3:1 makes a comment on this kind of reptile, saying: "Now the serpent [na·hhash'] proved to be the most cautious of all the wild beasts of the field that Jehovah God had made." So rather than lying in wait to do harm to a human, it was inclined to withdraw itself from contact with humans. But now, strangely, it was plainly observable, whether on the ground or on a tree. Why?

[5] "So," Genesis 3:1 goes on to say, "it began to say to the woman: 'Is it really so that God said you must not eat from every tree of the garden?' " Well, now, how had the serpent heard such a thing? Or how did it understand such a thing? Also, how is it that it had never before spoken to the woman's husband Adam? How is it that it could speak with human language at all? Never before had a serpent spoken to a human, and never has it done so since. Eve was not imagining that someone was speaking to her. She was not speaking to herself in her own mind, just thinking. The humanlike voice seemed to come from the mouth of the serpent. How could that be? The only other voice

---

3. Since God's desire was for mankind to keep on living in Paradise, what question is forced on us today?
4. Why was it strange for a serpent to make itself observable to a human in Paradise?
5. Why was it strange that the serpent asked Eve a question, and why was it not God's voice indirectly?

besides that of her husband Adam that Eve had heard in the garden was that of God, but directly, not through some subhuman animal creature. According to what the serpent, to all appearances, said, the voice was not that of God. The voice asked Eve about what God had said.

⁶ When Eve answered the question, she was speaking, not to that serpent, but to the invisible intelligence that was using the serpent like a ventriloquist. Was this invisible intelligent speaker friendly to God or otherwise? Certainly the method that the unseen speaker used in speaking to Eve was deceptive, leading her to think that it was the serpent that was doing the speaking. That inquiring speaker was hiding his identity behind a visible serpent and was thus acting deceitfully. However, Eve did not discern and appreciate that this serpent-using speaker was maliciously trying to deceive her. Unsuspectingly Eve made her reply.

"At this the woman said to the serpent: 'Of the fruit of the trees of the garden we may eat. But as for eating of the fruit of the tree that is in the middle of the garden, God has said, "You must not eat from it, no, you must not touch it that you do not die." ' "—Genesis 3:2, 3.

⁷ By designating it as "the tree that is in the middle of the garden," Eve meant the tree of the knowledge of good and bad. But how did Eve know about that tree? It must have been that Adam, as God's prophet, told her. He is the one to whom God said when Adam was by himself, before Eve's creation: "From every tree of the garden you may eat to satisfaction. But as for the tree of the knowledge of good and bad you must not eat from it, for in the day you eat from it you will positively die." (Genesis 2:16, 17) According to Eve, God also said not to touch the forbidden tree. So Eve was not ignorant of the penalty for violating God's law. It was death.

⁸ If the unseen speaker behind the serpent had been asking for mere information, he would have dropped the conversation on being given the information. Whether, at this time, the serpent was at the middle

6. In what way was the inquirer that used the serpent to put the question acting, and why did Eve reply?
7. Where did Eve get her information on the tree in the middle of the garden?
8. What shows whether the unseen inquirer was merely asking for information?

of the garden where the forbidden tree was located, and whether the serpent was on the ground or up the tree, is not stated. At least, the talk was about *that* "tree that is in the middle of the garden."

9 How could a mere serpent know or have authority to say what Eve now heard said? "At this the serpent said to the woman: 'You positively will not die. For God knows that in the very day of your eating from it your eyes are bound to be opened and you are bound to be like God, knowing good and bad.'"—Genesis 3:4, 5.

10 Here the unseen speaker behind the visible serpent was making himself a liar, for he was contradicting Jehovah God. For blatantly declaring that God had wrong motives in forbidding Adam and Eve's eating from the tree of the knowledge of good and bad, the unseen speaker was making himself a slanderer, a Devil, toward Jehovah God. He was not lovingly interested in eternal life for Eve, but was scheming to bring about her death. In fact, he was trying to remove the fear of death from her, not death at his hands, but death at the hands of Jehovah God for breaking his known command. The unseen speaker was setting himself in resistance to God and was in this manner making himself Satan, which means Resister. He was interested in getting someone else to resist God and put someone else on the side of Satan. We know who the real speaker of such a lie and slander was. It was no serpent!

11 Unhappily, Eve did not dispute this lying, slanderous statement. She did not lovingly and loyally come to the defense of her heavenly Father. She did not now recognize her husband Adam's headship over her and go to him to ask him whether he approved of her acting selfishly on the matter or not. He could have exposed the deception. But Eve let herself be thoroughly deceived. She entertained the wrong idea presented to her by a liar, slanderer and resister of God her heavenly Father. She let the fear of the terrible penalty for disobedience vanish. She let selfish desire begin forming in her heart. She let herself be drawn out by this desire

9, 10. How did the unseen speaker behind the serpent make a liar, a Devil, a Satan, of himself?
11. How did Eve now not show loyalty to God and respect for her husband, and let herself be tempted?

and enticed. God had said that it would be bad for her and Adam to eat the forbidden fruit, but she decided to establish for herself what was bad and what was good. She accordingly decided to prove her heavenly Father and God a liar. So now when Eve contemplated the tree, it became attractive-looking.

[12] "Consequently the woman saw that the tree was good for food and that it was something to be longed for to the eyes, yes, the tree was desirable to look upon. So she began taking of its fruit and eating it." (Genesis 3:6) In this way she became a transgressor against God, a sinner. The fact that she was thoroughly deceived did not excuse her. She lost her moral perfection.

[13] Her husband was not there to prevent her independent action. When she next joined him, she had to use persuasion to get him to eat, because he was in no way deceived. He did not choose to prove the one speaking by means of the serpent a liar and to vindicate Jehovah God as One using His universal sovereignty in a righteous manner, a beneficial manner. What, then, happened when Adam joined Eve in transgression? Genesis 3:6, 7 tells us:

"Afterward she gave some also to her husband when with her and he began eating it. Then the eyes of both of them became opened and they began to realize that they were naked. Hence they sewed fig leaves together and made loin coverings for themselves."

[14] They had now become "like God, knowing good and bad," in that they no longer accepted the standards of good and bad as set by Jehovah God but they had become judges for themselves as to what was good and what was bad. In spite of this, their consciences began to bother them. They felt exposed, needing a covering. Their bodily nakedness was no longer a clean, innocent state in their eyes, in which to appear before Jehovah God. So they began tailoring and covered over their private parts that God had given them for the honorable purpose of reproduction of their kind. Thus under the condemning testimony of their own consciences, they condemned themselves, even before the Sovereign Lord Jehovah did. Hence, we read:

---

12. By eating the forbidden fruit, what did Eve become, inexcusably?
13. By eating, what did Adam fail to do, with what effect on him?
14. What led Adam and Eve to condemn themselves before God did, and how did they act at his approach?

"Later they heard the voice of Jehovah God walking in the garden about the breezy part of the day, and the man and his wife went into hiding from the face of Jehovah God in between the trees of the garden. And Jehovah God kept calling to the man and saying to him: 'Where are you?' Finally he said: 'Your voice I heard in the garden, but I was afraid because I was naked and so I hid myself.' At that he said: 'Who told you that you were naked? From the tree from which I commanded you not to eat have you eaten?'"—Genesis 3:8-11.

¹⁵ Let us notice, now, that there is no expression of repentance on the part of Adam and Eve, but, rather, an effort to excuse themselves: Someone else was to blame. "And the man went on to say: 'The woman whom you gave to be with me, she gave me fruit from the tree and so I ate.' With that Jehovah God said to the woman: 'What is this you have done?' To this the woman replied: 'The serpent—it deceived me and so I ate.'" (Genesis 3:12, 13) However, excuses did not absolve these willful transgressors. But what about the serpent?

"And Jehovah God proceeded to say to the serpent: 'Because you have done this thing, you are the cursed one out of all the domestic animals and out of all the wild beasts of the field. Upon your belly you will go and dust is what you will eat all the days of your life. And I shall put enmity between you and the woman and between your seed and her seed. He will bruise you in the head and you will bruise him in the heel.'"—Genesis 3:14, 15, NW; Leeser; Zunz.

¹⁶ This was not a curse upon the whole serpent family. Seemingly God's words were addressed to that one literal serpent, but He knew that it had only been victimized to serve as an instrument of a superhuman, invisible spirit person, one who had hitherto been an obedient heavenly son of God. This one had also let himself be drawn out and enticed by a desire of a selfish kind. It was a desire for sovereignty over mankind, independent of Jehovah's universal sovereignty. This desire he had let take root in his heart and had cultivated it, till it became fertile and produced transgression, rebellion against the Sovereign Lord Jehovah. This spirit transgressor then made himself a liar, slanderer or Devil and a resister or Satan, right there at the Paradise of Pleasure.

¹⁷ As suggested by the abasement that was pro-

---

15. (a) What shows that there was no repentance on the part of Adam and Eve? (b) What did God then say to the serpent? 16, 17. (a) To whom did God's words to the serpent really apply? (b) To what did a first-century writer liken this abasement?

nounced upon that victimized serpent, God abased this newly risen Liar, Devil, Satan. One first-century Bible commentator likens this abasement to a 'throwing of Satan into Tartarus,' a disapproved state of spiritual darkness with no enlightenment from God.—2 Peter 2:4.

GOD'S ANOINTED ONE FORETOLD

[18] Here Jehovah God formed a new purpose, and he announced it. The lying Satan the Devil had risen up, and it now became God's purpose to raise up an Anointed One, a *Ma·shi'ahh* (Messiah) according to Adam's language. (Daniel 9:25) God spoke of this Anointed One, this Messiah, as the "seed" of "the woman." God would put enmity between this Anointed One and Satan the Devil, now symbolized by the serpent. This enmity would also extend itself to being between the Anointed One and the "seed" of the Great Serpent.

[19] The enmity foretold was to result in a battle that would have painful effects, but it would end with victory for the "seed" of "the woman." Like a snake that strikes at the heel of the leg (Genesis 49:17), the Great Serpent, Satan the Devil, would cause a heel wound to the woman's "seed." This heel wound would not prove fatal. It would be healed, to enable the woman's "seed" to bruise the Great Serpent in the head fatally. Thus the Great Serpent would perish, and his "seed" with him. A vital thing to be noted about this conflict is this: For the woman's "seed" to bruise and crush the head of the Great Serpent, Satan the Devil, the woman's "seed" would have to be a heavenly spirit person, not a mere human son of a woman on earth. Why so? Because the Great Serpent is a superhuman spirit person, a rebellious heavenly son of God. A mere human "seed" of an earthly woman would not be powerful enough to destroy the invisible Satan the Devil in the spirit realm. So the Anointed One of Jehovah's purpose must be a heavenly Messiah.

[20] Well, then, how about the "woman" whose "seed"

---

18. What new thing was here announced, with what features about it?
19. (a) In what conflict was this "enmity" to result? (b) Why would the Anointed One of Jehovah's purpose have to be heavenly?
20. Who, then, is the "woman" of Genesis 3:15?

the Anointed One or Messiah is? She, too, must be heavenly. Just as the serpent that was sentenced to being crushed in the head was not that literal serpent that had been used to deceive Eve, so the "woman" of Jehovah's prophecy in Genesis 3:15 was not a literal woman on earth. Eve was a personal transgressor against God's law and was an enticer of her husband Adam into transgression. So she herself was not worthy of being the personal mother of the promised "seed." The "woman" of God's prophecy must be a symbolic woman. It is just as when Jehovah God speaks of his chosen people as being his wife, his woman, saying to them: "Return, O backsliding children, saith the Lord; for I am become your husband." (Jeremiah 3:14; 31:31, *Leeser* [31:32, *NW*]) In a like manner God's heavenly organization of holy angels is as a wife to Jehovah God, and she is the heavenly mother of the "seed." She is "the woman." It is between this "woman" and the Serpent that God puts enmity.

ORIGINAL PURPOSE NOT TO BE A FAILURE

21 What, though, about God's purpose concerning the earth as stated to Adam and Eve at the close of the sixth creative "day"? Was it now to fail because of the transgression by Eve and Adam, meriting their being put to death? This original purpose was to have all the surface of the earth a Paradise, peopled by the descendants of the first, the original, man and woman on earth, Adam and Eve. Failure is a thing that could not happen with God's stated purpose. No Satan the Devil is able to cause God's purpose to fail and disgrace him. That God's original purpose was still to go forward to triumphant fulfillment is indicated in what was now said to the woman Eve by Jehovah God the Supreme Judge.

22 "To the woman he said: 'I shall greatly increase the pain of your pregnancy; in birth pangs you will bring forth children, and your craving will be for your husband, and he will dominate you.'" (Genesis 3:16) This signified that the producing of further inhabitants

---

21. Was God's original purpose concerning the earth now to fail because of the arising of transgression?
22. (a) Peopling of the earth by whom was to go ahead? (b) Was it reasonable to believe that bruising of the Serpent's head would result in benefit to mankind?

of the earth from this original human pair was to be permitted. It has continued till now, and today there is worrisome talk about a "population explosion." Since the Great Serpent, Satan the Devil, had induced the bringing of death upon all the descendants of the first human couple, evidently the bruising of the "head" of this Great Serpent was to result in benefit to those descendants who had been hurt by his transgression. Exactly how? That was something for Jehovah God to make plain in due course. This would work toward the success of His original purpose.

23 Now, finally, came the turn of the man, the third one in the order of transgression. God had told him that in the day in which he ate of the forbidden fruit he would positively die. (Genesis 2:17) For his wife Eve to bring forth children in birth pangs, it would require Adam to live on as her husband and father her children. So how was what God had warned him of carried out?

24 Genesis 3:17-19 makes clear how: "And to Adam he said: 'Because you listened to your wife's voice and took to eating from the tree concerning which I gave you this command, "You must not eat from it," cursed is the ground on your account. In pain you will eat its produce all the days of your life. And thorns and thistles it will grow for you, and you must eat the vegetation of the field. In the sweat of your face you will eat bread until you return to the ground, for out of it you were taken. For dust you are and to dust you will return.'" With those judicial words, Jehovah God pronounced the sentence of death upon the transgressor, and this within the same day in which Adam had transgressed.

25 Judicially, from God's standpoint, Adam died that very day, and his transgressing wife Eve did also. Cut off from them both was the opportunity and prospect of living forever in happiness in the Paradise of Pleasure. He was now dead in his own transgression. He could henceforth pass on to his offspring by Eve only a dying existence and condemnation, due to inherited human imperfection. All his offspring would

23-25. (a) When was the sentence of death pronounced upon Adam for his transgression? (b) In what way, then, was it that Adam died in the day that he ate the forbidden fruit, and what about his offspring?

have to say, as the psalmist David said thousands of years later: "Look! With error I was brought forth with birth pains, and in sin my mother conceived me." (Psalm 51:5) To all sinful mankind God can say, as he did to his chosen people: "Your own father, the first one, has sinned." (Isaiah 4͠:͠27) All mankind died in Adam on the day that the Supre.. ˼udge pronounced sentence upon him for his sin. A˼...˼am got his sentence, physical death was inescapable for him.

26 Quite appropriately, the "book of Adam's history" tells us: "He became father to sons and daughters. So all the days of Adam that he lived amounted to nine hundred and thirty years and he died." (Genesis 5:1-5) He lived seventy years less than a thousand years. None of his offspring have lived a full thousand years, the oldest one, Methuselah, living only nine hundred and sixty-nine years. (Genesis 5:27) Even from God's viewing a thousand years as one day, Adam died within the first thousand-year "day" of mankind's existence. Where did he go at his physical death? Not even his "soul" (*neph'esh*) had been taken from heaven, and he did not "return" there. He did return to the dust of the ground, because, as God said, from there Adam had been taken. He then ceased to be a "living soul." (Genesis 2:7) He ceased to exist. When his wife Eve died a physical death, she, too, ceased to be a "living soul." There was no soul to live on forever and ever according to the Babylonian religious mythology.

LOSS OF PARADISE

27 The wording of God's sentence upon Adam, especially the words about the "cursed . . . ground," meant that Adam was to lose Paradise. He did. Paradise was not cursed because of the transgression of Eve and Adam; it continued to be a place of life, still having within it the "tree of life." Genesis 3:20-24 informs us:

"After this Adam called his wife's name Eve, because she had to become the mother of everyone living. And Jehovah God proceeded to make long garments of skin for Adam and for his wife and to clothe them. And Jehovah God went on

26. Even when a "day" is viewed as a thousand years, how did Adam die on the day of his transgression, and what did he cease to be?
27. To what part of the earth did the cursing of the ground apply, and what did Adam's working cursed ground mean for him and Eve?

to say: 'Here the man has become like one of us in knowing good and bad, and now in order that he may not put his hand out and actually take fruit also from the tree of life and eat and live to time indefinite,—' With that Jehovah God put him out of the garden of Eden to cultivate the ground from which he had been taken. And so he drove the man out and posted at the east of the garden of Eden the cherubs and the flaming blade of a sword that was turning itself continually to guard the way to the tree of life."

²⁸ Having the power of death, Jehovah God put the man out of reach of the tree of life, in order to enforce the death penalty upon Adam. Adam's wife went along with her husband in order to become mother to his children. Whether God drove out the snake that had been used to tempt Eve, the record does not indicate. Life to time indefinite was no longer possible for Adam and Eve.

²⁹ There is no record that, outside the garden of Eden, Eve brought up her sons to hate snakes. But God's heavenly organization of holy angels, the true "woman" meant in God's prophecy of Genesis 3:15, immediately began to hate the Great Serpent, Satan the Devil. Love for Jehovah God as her heavenly husband prompted the womanlike organization to do so. God indeed placed enmity between His "woman" and the Great Serpent. When she was to bring forth the "seed" that would bruise the head of the Great Serpent lay within the purpose of Jehovah God. He had now formed his purpose in his Anointed One, his Messiah, and had made that fact known to heaven and earth, now almost six thousand years ago. That was ages of time ago. This added purpose reinforced God's original purpose regarding a Paradise earth and made certain its fulfillment. The unchangeable God still sticks to that announced purpose in his Anointed One, His Messiah. We can greatly rejoice that it is now triumphing for man's good.

---

28. Why was life to time indefinite no longer possible for Adam?
29. (a) How did God now put "enmity" between the "woman" and the "serpent"? (b) What effect did God's announced purpose have upon his original purpose for the earth, and why may we now rejoice?

CHAPTER 6

Human Life Outside Paradise Until the Deluge

IN THE process of time man's heavenly Benefactor made known a feature of his "eternal purpose" that strikes a sympathetic chord in our hearts. It was that the purposed "seed" of his heavenly "woman" would have a temporary existence on earth among mankind. This immediately raises the question in our minds, since the "seed" would be born into our human race, then through which line of descent from Adam and Eve would the "seed" come?

2 The history of the human line of descent of the "seed" is the important thing for us to know. The history of peoples and nations that have nothing to do with the life course of this "seed" is not indispensably important or valuable. That is why Jehovah God limited the contents of the Holy Bible mainly to telling us about the working out of the line of descent of this "seed." By our getting a knowledge of this Bible history we will be able to identify who this Serpent-bruising "seed" is, and we will not leave ourselves open to being deceived and misled by a pretender, a false seed. Deception could lead to eternal destruction for us. The Great Deceiver, who put lying deceit across in the garden of Eden and who is at enmity with the true "seed," is still at his old tricks. He would like to deceive all of us away from the "seed" of God's "eternal purpose." So we need to study the Bible.

3 In the Hebrew Bible, the two books of Chronicles are listed last, and not the prophetic book of Malachi. Now, if we turn to the first book of Chronicles we notice that it opens up with a line of ten generations after Adam, as follows: "Adam, [1] Seth, [2] Enosh,

---

1. What feature about the "seed" of his purpose did God make known, this raising what question?
2. To what mainly did God limit the contents of the Bible, and why do we need to study the Bible?
3. Who was Adam's firstborn son, and so what question is raised about Adam's son Seth?

[3] Kenan, [4] Mahalalel, [5] Jared, [6] Enoch, [7] Methuselah, [8] Lamech, [9] Noah, [10] Shem, Ham and Japheth." (1 Chronicles 1:1-4) Seth was not the first-born son of Adam outside the Paradise of Pleasure. Cain was, and Abel was the next-named son of Adam and Eve. (Genesis 4:1-5) Why, then, was Seth made the one to be listed in the line of descent down to Noah?

⁴ Did Jehovah God plan it that way? No, for that would mean that God planned that Cain should murder his younger brother Abel and thus disqualify himself from being the one through whom mankind today could trace its descent. Neither did God plan that, by foul murder, Abel should be cut off prematurely before having the needed offspring and that thus Seth should be substituted for him. (Genesis 4:25) That God did not plan the murdering of Abel in order to make room for Seth is evident from the warning that God gave to Cain that he might not fall victim to gross sin because of resenting it that his offering to God had been rejected but his brother Abel's sacrifice had been accepted.—Genesis 4:6, 7.

⁵ No, Jehovah God did not plan it that way, but it took a long time before there was born a son of Adam through whom the line of descent would run down clear to the birth of the promised "seed," the Messiah, in the flesh. This lateness of beginning the favored line of descent from Adam is shown in Genesis 5:3, where we read: "And Adam lived on for a hundred and thirty years. Then he became father to a son in his likeness, in his image, and called his name Seth." Being in Adam's likeness and image, or, being of Adam's kind, Seth was imperfect, having inherited sin and hence being under condemnation of death. The realization of this fact appears to be borne out in the name that Seth gave to his son, concerning whom we read: "And to Seth also there was born a son and he proceeded to call his name Enosh." (Genesis 4:26) The name has the sense of "sickly, morbid, incurable."

⁶ In harmony with this the Hebrew word *e·nosh'*, when not used as a proper name, is translated as "mor-

----

4. What shows that God did not *plan* that Seth should be the first one listed in the line of descent from Adam?
5, 6. Seth's being born in Adam's likeness and image meant what for him, and how does naming his son Enosh show realization of this fact?

tal man." For instance, when the sorely afflicted Job says: "What is mortal man [Hebrew: *e·nosh'*] that you should rear him, and that you should set your heart upon him?"—See Job 7:17; 15:14; also, Psalm 8:4; 55:13; 144:3; Isaiah 8:1.

⁷ The lifetime of Adam's grandson Enosh was marked by something notable, to which Genesis 4:26 calls our attention, saying with reference to the birth of Enosh to Seth: "At that time a start was made of calling on the name of Jehovah." Enosh was born when Seth was one hundred and five years old, which would mean two hundred and thirty-five years after Adam's creation. (Genesis 5:6, 7) By then the human population of the earth had increased by the marriage of Adam's many sons and daughters among themselves and by the marriages of their offspring. Was this starting to 'call on the name of Jehovah' among this growing population something favorable to humankind and honoring to God? Was it what modern-day evangelists would likely call a "religious revival"? The ancient Greek *Septuagint Version,* made by Jews of Alexandria, Egypt, translates this Hebrew passage: "And Seth had a son, and he called his name Enos: he hoped to call on the name of the Lord God."—Genesis 4:26, *LXX,* edition of S. Bagster and Sons Limited.

⁸ The *Jerusalem Bible* translation expresses a similar thought, saying: "This man was the first to invoke the name of Yahweh." But such a translation leaves out of consideration the acceptable worship that the faithful Abel rendered to Jehovah before he was murdered by jealous Cain. As for *The New English Bible,* it reads: "At that time men began to invoke the Lᴏʀᴅ by name." (Also, *The New American Bible*) However, the ancient Palestinian Targum takes an unfavorable view of the matter. The famous Rashi (Rabbi Shelomoh Yitschaki, of 1040-1105 C.E.) renders Genesis 4:26: "Then was the profane called by the Name of the Lord." That is to say, men and inanimate objects had attributed to them the qualities of Jehovah and were called accordingly. This would mean that idolatry in the name of Jehovah began then.

⁹ That the calling on the name of Jehovah was not

7-9. (a) What religious practice was started in the days of Enosh? (b) What indicates whether this practice was beneficial for man or not?

in a Godward sense is indicated in the fact that it was not until three hundred and eighty-seven years after the birth of Enosh that a man was born who received the recognition of God. This was Enoch.

WALKING WITH GOD OUTSIDE PARADISE

[10] Concerning this great-great-grandson of Enosh, who was born in 3404 B.C.E. (or 622 A.M.), it is written: "And Enoch lived on for sixty-five years. Then he became father to Methuselah. And after his fathering Methuselah Enoch went on walking with the true God three hundred years. Meanwhile he became father to sons and daughters. So all the days of Enoch amounted to three hundred and sixty-five years." (Genesis 5:21-23) This was a comparatively short life for Enoch, whose father Jared lived for nine hundred and sixty-two years and whose son Methuselah lived nine hundred and sixty-nine years to become the oldest man on record. And yet Enoch was "walking with the true God." This was not said of his father Jared, who lived on eight hundred years after the birth of Enoch. (Genesis 5:18, 19) Evidently, then, Jared's faith did not compare with Enoch's faith in God and he did not walk according to God's will or announced purpose.

[11] It is reliably reported that Enoch was a prophet of the True God. In a letter written in the first century C.E., it is written: "Yes, the seventh one in line from Adam, Enoch, prophesied also regarding them, when he said: 'Look! Jehovah came with his holy myriads, to execute judgment against all, and to convict all the ungodly concerning all their ungodly deeds that they did in an ungodly way, and concerning all the shocking things that ungodly sinners spoke against him.'" (Jude 14, 15) This prophecy no doubt reflects on the religious condition that existed back there in Enoch's day. Otherwise, what would be the basis for the giving of such an inspired prophecy that warned of Jehovah's coming judgment against all the ungodly that was as sure as if it had already occurred? Because Enoch was not one of the ungodly of his day, God could use him as a speaker of prophecy. Although living outside the

10. Its being said that Enoch walked with the true God reflected how on his longer-living father Jared?
11. What prophecy did Enoch give, and on what condition of the people must this have reflected?

cherub-guarded Paradise that still existed in Enoch's day, he "went on walking with the true God."

12 Why is it, then, that Enoch lived such a comparatively short life for those times? Genesis 5:24 informs us: "And Enoch kept walking with the true God. Then he was no more, for God took him."

13 Likely Enoch was in some dire predicament when God took him. Was it that Enoch's enemies threatened to kill him, and so God took him off the scene to spare him from a violent death? We do not know. The question arises, Where did God take him? Some Jewish thought is that God took him to heaven. That is even the thought in Christendom today. For instance, in a letter written to the Hebrews in the first century C.E., a comment is made upon Enoch and this is the way that the *A New Translation of The Bible*, by Dr. James Moffatt, of this century, renders Hebrews 11:5, as follows: "It was by faith that Enoch was taken to heaven, so that he never died (*he was not overtaken by death, for God had taken him away*)." *The New English Bible* reads here: "By faith Enoch was carried away to another life without passing through death; he was not to be found, because God had taken him. For it is the testimony of Scripture that before he was taken he had pleased God."—See, also, *The Jerusalem Bible*.

14 However, Psalm 89:48 asks the question: "What able-bodied man is there alive who will not see death? Can he provide escape for his soul from the hand of Sheol?" So, too, Enoch had received from sinner Adam the inheritance of death, and he too was obliged to die, despite his walking with the true God. It was later written of Enoch's great-grandson that this one also "walked with the true God"; and yet this latter one did not have his life cut short. He lived longer than Adam—for nine hundred and fifty years, fifty short of a thousand years. (Genesis 6:9; 9:28, 29) Consequently, Enoch's walking with God for less time than did his great-grandson did not entitle him to go to heaven or to another life any more than Noah's walking with God for so long entitled him to such an experience.

12, 13. According to Jewish thought, and that of Christendom, where was Enoch taken?
14. What shows whether 'walking with God' entitled Enoch to be taken to heaven?

¹⁵ The prophet Moses died at one hundred and twenty years of age and God buried him, so that no man to this day knows where Moses lies buried. (Deuteronomy 34:5-7) So God suddenly removed Enoch from the scene of his contemporaries, and where Enoch died is not known, or any grave. He did not die a violent death at the hand of his enemies. He being a prophet, it could be that while he was in a prophetic trance he had a vision of God's new order of things in which God "will actually swallow up death forever." (Isaiah 25:8) In that new order Enoch expected to live on a Paradise earth. While Enoch was under the power of such a vision of where mankind will be relieved of death by God's merciful provision, God could have removed him off the scene and terminated his present life, so that Enoch was not aware of dying. In such a marvelous way it would be fulfilled what is written in Hebrews 11:5:

"By faith Enoch was transferred so as not to see death, and he was nowhere to be found because God had transferred him; for before his transference he had the witness that he had pleased God well."—*New World Translation of the Holy Scriptures.*

THE DAYS BEFORE THE DELUGE

¹⁶ Enoch's son Methuselah was born 969 years before the global deluge, and so he died in the year of the Deluge. Although Methuselah was the eighth in the line counted from Adam, did he know Adam his first human parent? Yes. Adam was created 1,656 years before the Deluge. He lived 930 years. If we add his age to that of Methuselah, it comes to 1,899 years. By subtracting 1,656 years from that total, it results in 243 years. So the lives of Adam and Methuselah overlapped upon each other for 243 years.—Genesis 5:5, 21, 25-27.

¹⁷ Methuselah lived long enough to hear the warnings proclaimed about the coming global deluge, and he almost saw the completion of the preparations made for some of humankind to survive that world catastrophe. He was able to see his grandson Noah preaching righteousness and preparing the means for human survival. Of all of Methuselah's sons, Lamech was the

15. How, then, may Enoch have been transferred so as not to see death?
16. How do we figure that Adam and Methuselah knew each other?
17. What prophecy did Methuselah's son Lamech utter at the birth of Noah, and why was this name appropriate?

one who became the father of Noah. It was at the birth of Noah that Lamech was inspired to utter a prophecy concerning him. That disclosed that God purposed to use Lamech's son Noah. On this we read: "And Lamech lived on for a hundred and eighty-two years. Then he became father to a son. And he proceeded to call his name Noah, saying: 'This one will bring us comfort from our work and from the pain of our hands resulting from the ground which Jehovah has cursed.'" Lamech lived on to within five years of the Deluge. (Genesis 5:27-31) The name Noah was in harmony with Lamech's prophecy, for it means "Rest" and implies consolation from rest. God's curse was to be lifted from the ground that He had cursed on account of Adam's transgression.—Genesis 3:17.

[18] The deluge came within the sixth hundredth year of Noah's life and continued into his six hundred and first year of life. (Genesis 7:11; 8:13; 7:6) The world catastrophe that occurred in Noah's day foreshadowed the larger world catastrophe that is shortly to occur within our generation, and for this reason it deserves our consideration.—Proverbs 22:3.

[19] For centuries Noah, born in 2970 B.C.E. (1056 A.M.), was childless: "And Noah got to be five hundred years old. After that Noah became father to Shem, Ham and Japheth." (Genesis 5:32) What kind of record did Noah make for himself, even before becoming a father? "This is the history of Noah. Noah was a righteous man. He proved himself faultless among his contemporaries. Noah walked with the true God." (Genesis 6:9, 10) So Noah was like Enoch.

[20] Even though Noah was a descendant of Seth and Enoch and also "walked with the true God," yet Noah was not called a 'son of the true God.' If he was not thus called, who else on earth in those days of descent from sinner Adam could be thus called? Who, then, were those who were reported as appearing on earth in the days of Noah, concerning whom we now read? "Now it came about that when men started to grow in numbers on the surface of the ground and daughters were born to them, then the sons of the true God

18. When, in Noah's life, did the deluge start, and thereafter end?
19. How was Noah like Enoch in his course of life?
20. Why does a question arise regarding "sons of the true God" reported on the earth in Noah's days?

began to notice the daughters of men, that they were good-looking; and they went taking wives for themselves, namely, all whom they chose. After that Jehovah said: 'My spirit shall not act toward man indefinitely in that he is also flesh. Accordingly his days shall amount to a hundred and twenty years.' "—Genesis 6:1-3.

21 Those "sons of the true God" must have been angels from heaven, who up till this time had been part of Jehovah's heavenly organization of holy "sons of the true God," Jehovah's symbolic "woman" that was to become the mother of the promised "seed." At the founding of the earth for human habitation, they had observed Jehovah's creative work and had shouted in applause. (Job 38:7; Genesis 3:15) Observing marriage practiced among mankind, especially involving good-looking womenfolk, they let themselves go to desiring sex life on earth with women for themselves.

22 How could they as spirit creatures enjoy sex relations with women of flesh on earth? By materializing in fleshly bodies as desirable men and taking human wives and having sexual intercourse with them. As the Creator and heavenly Father had authorized marriage between fleshly earthly creatures of like nature and not between spirit creatures and fleshly human creatures, these "sons of the true God" did not come and materialize as men of flesh in order to serve as messengers of Jehovah God, commissioned and sent by Him. They proceeded to cause a confusion of natures— spirit and human, heavenly and earthly. (Leviticus 18:22, 23) Manifestly those "sons of the true God" were sinning.

23 By now more than a thousand years had passed since Adam's rebellion in Eden against the universal sovereignty of Jehovah God. Jehovah had acted with the spirit of patience and forbearance toward sinful mankind, for even in the days of Noah's great-grandfather Enoch mankind in general had become notoriously "ungodly." And now they were entering

21. Who were those "sons of the true God," and what did they go to desiring?
22. How did those "sons of the true God" satisfy their desire and thereby sin?
23. With what spirit had God long acted toward sinful mankind, but what did he now declare?

into a new form of moral corruption and sex perversion by marriages between women and materialized angels. The time deserved to come when the patient Creator should cease to act toward self-degrading mankind with a spirit of toleration and self-restraint. Fully justified, God finally declared: "My spirit shall not act toward man indefinitely in that he is also flesh. Accordingly his days shall amount to a hundred and twenty years."—Genesis 6:3.

²⁴ That was not a setting of an age limit upon man as in the case of the prophet Moses, who lived to be a hundred and twenty years old. It was a divine decree that the ungodly world of mankind should have only one hundred and twenty years more to exist until the global deluge. So this divine decree was published in 1536 A.M. or 2490 B.C.E. This meant that there the "time of the end" had begun for that ungodly world of Noah's days. The God of purpose was timing matters. Although he had not planned for such a shocking thing happening in the case of the "sons of the true God," yet he was still in full control and could handle the contingency. He is all-wise, almighty. His allowing such an extended time period before the end of that ungodly world was very considerate. Why? Because the divine decree was issued twenty years before Noah became a father and yet it allowed for him to have three sons and for these to grow up and get married and to join their father in making due preparations for surviving the threatening deluge.—Genesis 5:32; 7:11.

THE NEPHILIM

²⁵ The days of the intermarriage between passionate "sons of the true God" and women were numbered. But was any offspring possible from this confusion of natures between materialized spirits and fleshly female creatures with procreative powers? Genesis 6:4 gives us the facts in answer:

"The Nephilim proved to be in the earth in those days, and also after that, when the sons of the true God continued to have relations with the daughters of men and they bore sons

24. (a) Was God there setting man's age limit, as in Moses' case? (b) What then set in, and why was there a generous time allowance?
25, 26. What were the offspring of the marriages of angels and women called, and why?

to them, they were the mighty ones who were of old, the men of fame."

26 The sons of these mixed marriages were hybrids and were called Nephilim. This name means "Fellers," to indicate that these mighty hybrid sons violently felled others or caused weaker humans to fall. It took considerable time for these Nephilim to be conceived and born and then grow up to set out on their violent career. Being hybrids, they normally would not be able to reproduce their mixed kind.

27 The human family was not benefited by the intermingling of disobedient materialized "sons of the true God" so intimately with humans. "Consequently Jehovah saw that the badness of man was abundant in the earth and every inclination of the thoughts of his heart was only bad all the time. And Jehovah felt regrets that he had made men in the earth, and he felt hurt at his heart. So Jehovah said: 'I am going to wipe men whom I have created off the surface of the ground, from man to domestic animal, to moving animal and to flying creature of the heavens, because I do regret that I have made them.' But Noah found favor in the eyes of Jehovah." (Genesis 6:5-8) Jehovah regretted that man whom He had created had sunk so low morally and spiritually. It was regrettable to have men of such degraded personalities on the earth. These were the ones whom He purposed to wipe off the earth, but not the human race of which Noah was a righteous member.

28 In glaring contrast with Noah and his family, "the earth came to be ruined in the sight of the true God and the earth became filled with violence. So God saw the earth and, look! it was ruined, because all flesh had ruined its way on the earth." (Genesis 6:11, 12) In those days before the Deluge the world of mankind had entered an age of violence. Today the world has entered an "age of violence," as observers call it, ever since the year 1914 C.E., the year in which World War I let loose with all its violence. So we might well ask, What would the condition of the world be today if Almighty God had let that "age of violence"

27. What was it that God purposed to wipe off the face of the earth, and why?
28. Why can we today be thankful that God purposed to end that pre-Deluge state of violence on the earth?

before the Deluge continue on without interruption?
It makes us shudder to think of the possibilities. Long
before now the earth would have been a place too
dangerous to live in. We can be thankful that God
purposed to halt that pre-Deluge "age of violence."

A WORLD ENDS, A RACE SURVIVES

29 Jehovah God stuck to his original purpose to have
the earth fully inhabited by the descendants of the first
man and woman amid Paradise conditions. Also, the
line of descent that would lead up to the producing
of the Messiah needed to be preserved. In keeping
with this, Jehovah instructed obedient Noah to build
an ark (or, a floating chest) of such capacity as to
contain Noah and his family and basic specimens of
the land animals and flying creatures of the heavens
like the dove and the raven. No room in the ark was
occupied by a steam engine or a diesel engine and
fuel supplies in order to propel the ark somewhere; it
just floated, with its living occupants and food supplies
sufficient for a year or more.—Genesis 6:13–7:18.

30 To understand the possibilities for such a planetary
flood of water, we have to visualize the state of things
with regard to our globe as a whole. At its surface
there were landmasses, large and small, sticking up
above the seas. Up above all of this there was a vault
or expanse containing the atmosphere that mankind
and other living creatures breathed. But out beyond
this there was a deep watery canopy that surrounded
the earth like a swaddling band and that the Creator
had caused to be lifted up to a scientifically accurate
height on the second creative "day." There it remained
in suspension like an envelope around the earthly
globe, to collapse back to the earth only according to
the Creator's purpose and at His command. (Genesis
1:6-8) An inspired Bible commentator of the first century C.E. nicely described it, saying: "There were heavens from of old and an earth standing compactly out
of water and in the midst of water by the word of
God."—2 Peter 3:5, NW; Jerusalem Bible.

29. Jehovah's instructions to Noah harmonized with what purpose
of God for the earth?
30. To make possible such a planetary flood, what was the natural
state at and around the earth since the second creative "day"?

³¹ The global deluge is no myth that stems from Babylonish sources. It is a historical fact that has left its effects on the earth to this day. It was dated and timed. According to Noah's ship log or ark log, it began on the seventeenth day of the second month of the lunar year, in the six hundredth year of his life.

³² Then Noah logged the precipitation of water from the skies as continuing for forty days. Even the tops of the then mountains were covered with floodwaters to a depth of fifteen cubits. On the seventeenth day of the seventh lunar month the ark touched ground at the mountains of Ararat. According to the Creator's power, new basins were formed in the outer crust of the earthly globe to drain off the floodwaters. On the first day of the first month of the new lunar year the draining process was completed. On the twenty-seventh day of the second month of the new lunar year, or one lunar year and ten days after the deluge began, God told Noah to leave the ark and let all the animal life therein also go forth.—Genesis 7:11 through 8:19.

³³ In this way, under divine protection, the human race from Adam survived the global deluge, but an ungodly world or a world of ungodly people came to an end. This meant also that those infamous hybrid Nephilim were destroyed, they being fleshly like all the rest of mankind. In simple, understandable language the inspired first-century Bible commentator correctly described it, saying:

"He [God] did not hold back from punishing an ancient world, but kept Noah, a preacher of righteousness, safe with seven others when he brought a deluge upon a world of ungodly people; . . . by those means the world of that time suffered destruction when it was deluged with water."—2 Peter 2:5; 3:6.

³⁴ This agrees with the statement of the prophet Moses: "Everything in which the breath of the force of life was active in its nostrils, namely, all that were on the dry ground, died. Thus he wiped out every existing thing that was on the surface of the ground, from man to beast, to moving animal and to flying creature of the heavens, and they were wiped off the earth;

31, 32. What did Noah's statistics show regarding the deluge?
33. What perished in the Deluge, and what survived?
34. According to Moses, what happened to living creatures on the earth and to those in the ark?

and only Noah and those who were with him in the ark kept on surviving. And the waters continued overwhelming the earth a hundred and fifty days."—Genesis 7:22-24.

35 This deluge on a global scale was indeed an "act of God." It dramatically illustrates a point that we of today ought to take to heart. What point? "Jehovah knows how to deliver people of godly devotion out of trial, but to reserve unrighteous people for the day of judgment to be cut off." (2 Peter 2:9) "Everything Jehovah has made for his purpose, yes, even the wicked one for the evil day." (Proverbs 16:4) So, then, if we do not desire to be reserved for the fast-approaching "evil day," Jehovah's own-timed "day" for executing his righteous judgments against all unrighteous persons on earth, it behooves us to 'walk with God,' as Noah did, and conform to His purpose.

36 At the Deluge, not just unrighteous men and Nephilim had divine judgment carried out against them, but those disobedient "sons of God" also experienced a deserved judgment against them. True, when the Deluge overwhelmed the whole earth, those "sons of the true God" left their wives and families and dematerialized and did not drown. But what about when they returned to their spirit condition, which was their own proper dwelling place? Did they then resume the former intimacy that they had had with God? Was their relationship with Him the same as before? Did they continue in his holy heavenly organization as still being "sons of the true God"? No; but in these disobedient spirit creatures we see the origin of the "demons" (aside from Satan the Devil) that the prophet Moses speaks about. (Deuteronomy 32:17; also Psalm 106:37) But the first-century Bible commentators are more specific as to how Jehovah God dealt with those disobedient spirits, saying:

"The angels that did not keep their original position but forsook their own proper dwelling place he has reserved with eternal bonds under dense darkness for the judgment of the great day." (Jude 6) "The spirits in prison, who had once been disobedient when the patience of God was waiting in Noah's days, while the ark was being constructed, in which

35. If we do not want to be reserved for the "evil day" of God's judgment execution, what should we now do, like Noah?
36. (a) At the Deluge, what happened to the Nephilim? (b) Also, what consequences did the disobedient "sons of the true God" undergo?

a few people, that is, eight souls, were carried safely through the water." (1 Peter 3:19, 20) "God did not hold back from punishing the angels that sinned, but, by throwing them into Tartarus, delivered them to pits of dense darkness to be reserved for judgment."—2 Peter 2:4.

[37] So the dematerializing of the disobedient "sons of the true God" and their return to the spirit realm did not transform them into holy angels once again. They found themselves on the side of Satan the Devil, the original rebel against Jehovah God. They were no longer fit for a place in Jehovah's wifelike heavenly organization of holy, obedient "sons of the true God." For this reason they were degraded to the status of "demons." This low, dishonored state was appropriately spoken of as Tartarus, a name borrowed from the Greek language. The Syriac Bible version speaks of it as "the lowest places." (See also Job 40:15; 41:23 in the Greek *Septuagint Version*.) Those disobedient spirits were no more favored with spiritual enlightenment such as God saw fit to bestow upon his faithful angelic sons. In this way they were plunged into dense darkness and were held there as if by "eternal bonds," to be reserved for the "judgment of the great day." So they can impart no real enlightenment to mankind.

[38] Such disobedient spirits became the invisible "seed" of the Great Serpent, Satan the Devil. Their being put into Tartarean "pits of dense darkness" along with Satan the Devil was not a bruising of the serpent's head by the promised "seed" of God's heavenly "woman." The holy "seed" had not yet been produced, and those imprisoned wicked spirits were anxious to know who it would be in order that they might join in bruising the "heel" of that "seed." (Genesis 3:15) For that reason those wicked spirits under Satan their chief kept close to humankind, to deceive them and turn them against the "seed" when it should arrive. They try to communicate with humans through spirit mediums, since they themselves are debarred from further materializing in the flesh. They pretend to be the "disembodied souls" of deceased humans. They obsess or beset and besiege weak-minded persons, and even take possession of yielding persons. The prophet

---

37. On their returning to the spirit realm, what did the status of the disobedient "sons of the true God" come to be?
38. Whose "seed" did those disobedient spirits become, and how do they operate to man's deception and enslavement?

Moses was inspired to warn God's people against having anything to do with these demonic enemies of God. (Deuteronomy 18:9-13) So beware of spiritism!

39 Since we desire to receive enlightenment on the "eternal purpose" of Jehovah God, we need to avoid those spiritistic powers of darkness that blind the majority of mankind to God's truth. God's written Word, the Holy Bible, is the channel of spiritual illumination for us, according to the inspired words of the psalmist, when he said to Jehovah God: "Your word is a lamp to my foot, and a light to my roadway." —Psalm 119:105.

40 In the light of God's Word we have looked back over the first 1,656 years of man's existence on earth, from Adam's creation until the deluge of Noah's day. Despite the rebellion of both angels and men, the changeless God stuck to his first-formed purpose regarding mankind on earth. Though unstated numbers of angels yielded to selfish desire and sinned and needed to be expelled from his heavenly wifelike organization, these do not compare with those who remained faithful to Him within his holy organization, like a faithful wife to a loving husband. Millenniums afterward the prophet Daniel saw in vision a hundred million loyal angels still ministering to the Most High God, "the Ancient of Days." (Daniel 7:9, 10) This heavenly "woman," the prospective mother of the foretold "seed," was set at "enmity" with the Great Serpent, Satan the Devil, and his "seed." She was firmly determined to cooperate with Jehovah God in the pursuit of his newly announced purpose to produce the "seed" at his chosen time.

41 On earth and in the Paradise of Pleasure, Adam and Eve had been made a visible part of Jehovah's universal organization at their creation in human perfection. Under temptation they did not keep their integrity toward their Creator, their heavenly Father. Under sentence of death they were expelled from Jehovah's universal organization and ceased to be

---

39. If not to demons, then to what should we turn for spiritual enlightenment?
40. Despite rebellion of men and angels, what is there to show for loyalty on the part of God's heavenly organization and its cooperation?
41. What point did Satan maliciously aim to prove before all creation, and did he succeed completely even before the Deluge?

counted as children of His. But what of their offspring? To judge from integrity-breaking Adam and Eve, their imperfectly born, sin-inheriting offspring would be unable to maintain integrity to the Creator under temptation and pressure by the Great Serpent, Satan the Devil. Manifestly, Satan the Devil aimed to prove before all creation in heaven and earth that none of them would do so. Did he prove his point, even before the Deluge? The Bible record that expresses God's viewpoint on the subject shows that at least three men maintained their integrity, namely, Abel, Enoch and Noah.

⁴² Those three faithful, God-fearing men upheld the universal sovereignty of Jehovah their Creator. They proved that Satan the Devil is a presumptuous liar in arguing that Almighty God cannot put a man on earth that, even in a Paradise environment, will keep integrity to Jehovah when subjected to Satan the Devil's temptations and pressures. The cases of Abel, Enoch and Noah prove that God the Creator was justified in letting the human race, descended from the sinful Adam and Eve, continue to exist on earth. Other men, besides women, in addition to Abel, Enoch and Noah were sure to appear in the ranks of mankind as human life on earth went on outside Paradise, thus piling up more proof against the Devil's lie and slander against God.

⁴³ Jehovah's foresight was accurate, and his purpose was bound to succeed. His Messianic purpose that was announced in the presence of the Great Serpent in the garden of Eden added strength to God's original purpose and made sure its fulfillment. God's universal sovereignty over the earth, as demonstrated so mightily in the global deluge, will never cease over mankind.

42, 43. (a) The cases of Abel, Enoch and Noah established what proof? (b) How was Jehovah's foresight accurate with regard to the providing of further proof?

CHAPTER 7

Tracing the Human Line of Descent of the "Seed"

L YING at the heart of God's "eternal purpose" is the "seed" to be produced by God's "woman." The contest that began in the garden of Eden between Satan and God centered on this mysterious "seed." This had to be so, because that "seed" was to be brought forth in due time to bruise the head of the Great Serpent, and Satan the Devil knew that the "head" meant was his own. (Genesis 3:15) Satan was determined to break the integrity of the coming "seed" and thereby make him unfit for God's purpose. At the Deluge the first round of the contest between Satan and God was over, but with a showing against Satan. He had failed to crack the integrity of at least three men who were descended from the first man and woman whose integrity he had schemed to ruin. Abel, Enoch and Noah had weakened the confident position of Satan and had made him more desperate in his aim to wreck the "seed."

2 The next six hundred and fifty-eight years after the Deluge ended were to prove very revealing concerning details about the "seed" of God's "woman." After the deluge all mankind down till today could trace its descent from Noah the builder of the ark that weathered the deluge. So now the world of mankind was given a righteous start, for Noah "walked with the true God." (Genesis 6:9) Imperfect he was by heredity, but, morally, he was faultless, blameless, before God. How thankful we, his descendants, should be for that! Right after leaving the ark and setting foot on Mount Ararat, Noah led mankind in the worship of mankind's Preserver, Jehovah God.

1. Why had the cases of Abel, Enoch and Noah made Satan the Devil more desperate in his aim to wreck the promised "seed"?
2. Mankind today should be thankful that Noah gave them what kind of a start in life after the deluge? How so?

"Noah began to build an altar to Jehovah and to take some of all the clean beasts and of all the clean flying creatures and to offer burnt offerings upon the altar. And Jehovah began to smell a restful odor, and so Jehovah said in his heart: 'Never again shall I call down evil upon the ground on man's account, because the inclination of the heart of man is bad from his youth up; and never again shall I deal every living thing a blow just as I have done. For all the days the earth continues, seed sowing and harvest, and cold and heat, and summer and winter, and day and night, will never cease.'"—Genesis 8:20-22; compare Isaiah 54:9.

³ The prophecy that Noah's father Lamech pronounced over him at his birth proved to be justified. (Genesis 5:29) The divine curse pronounced upon the ground outside the garden of Eden after Adam's transgression was lifted, and Noah (whose name means "Rest") caused a restful odor to ascend from his burnt offerings to God and induced God's calling for a rest for mankind from the toil of cultivating a cursed ground. God also caused the first reported rainbow to appear in the light of the sun now shining directly upon the earth because of removal of the water canopy. Referring to that rainbow as a sign of guarantee, Jehovah promised that "no more will the waters become a deluge to bring all flesh to ruin." No more will there be a watery deluge.—Genesis 9:8-15.

⁴ Noah's three sons, Shem, Ham and Japheth, and their wives survived with him and his wife. Which one, now, of these three sons was to be the one through whom the line of descent would run down to the earthly appearance of the "seed" of God's "woman"? The choice that had to be made would affect differently the three races that would descend from the three patriarchs, Shem, Ham and Japheth. The prophecy that God inspired Noah to pronounce over his three sons on a critical occasion set forth in which way the divine favor and blessing would go. What was the basis for this?

⁵ In obedience to God's command to Noah's sons to become fruitful in the earth, Shem became father to

---

3. How did Lamech's prophecy at Noah's birth prove true, and of what did the rainbow become a symbol?
4. Noah's three sons and their wives having survived the deluge with Noah, what question now arose as to the promised "seed"?
5. What caused Noah to pronounce a curse upon Ham's son Canaan?

Arpachshad two years after the start of the deluge. (Genesis 11:10) In time Ham became father to Canaan. (Genesis 9:18; 10:6) Some time after Canaan's birth there was an occasion when Noah, for some unstated reason, got drunk on wine from his vineyard. Ham entered Noah's tent and saw him lying uncovered, naked, but he did nothing to conceal his father's nakedness. Rather, he aired it to Shem and Japheth. With due respect for their father, Shem and Japheth refused to look upon Noah's nakedness, and moving with their backs turned to their father, they spread a cloth over him. They took no advantage of their father's nakedness and showed and kept their high respect for him as their father and as Jehovah's prophet.

"Finally Noah awoke from his wine and got to know what his youngest son had done to him. At this he said: 'Cursed be Canaan. Let him become the lowest slave to his brothers.' And he added: 'Blessed be Jehovah, Shem's God, and let Canaan become a slave to him. Let God grant ample space to Japheth, and let him reside in the tents of Shem. Let Canaan become a slave to him also.' "—Genesis 9:20-27.

⁶ Noah was sober when he pronounced those words. He did not curse the whole race that descended from Ham, because of Ham's lack of respect, especially for God's prophet. So God inspired Noah to curse only one son of Ham, namely, Canaan, whose descendants took up residence in the land of Canaan in Palestine. The Canaanites did become slaves to the descendants of Shem, when God brought the Israelites into Canaanland in accord with His promise to Abraham the Hebrew. Shem lived five hundred and two years after the start of the Deluge, so that his life overlapped on that of Abraham by one hundred and fifty years. (Genesis 11:10, 11) Noah declared Jehovah to be Shem's God. Jehovah was to be blessed, because it was the fear of Him that motivated Shem to show the due respect for Noah as God's prophet. Japheth was to be treated as a guest in Shem's tents, and not as a slave like Canaan. Thus, by being a host to his brother Japheth, Shem was ranked as superior to him in the wording of the prophecy. In harmony with this, Shem's line of descent was to lead to Messiah.

6. According to Noah's prophecy, through which son was the line of descent to the Messiah to run?

THE FOUNDING OF BABYLON

7 Another descendant of Ham that did not turn out well was his grandson Nimrod. Surviving for three hundred and fifty years after the start of the deluge, Noah lived to see the rise and doubtless the downfall of this great-grandson of his. (Genesis 9:28, 29) Nimrod founded an organization that acted like part of the visible "seed" of the Great Serpent, Satan the Devil. Says Genesis 10:8-12: "And Cush became father to Nimrod. He made the start in becoming a mighty one in the earth. He displayed himself a mighty hunter in opposition to Jehovah. That is why there is a saying: 'Just like Nimrod a mighty hunter in opposition to Jehovah.' And the beginning of his kingdom came to be Babel and Erech and Accad and Calneh, in the land of Shinar. Out of that land he went forth into Assyria and set himself to building Nineveh and Rehoboth-Ir and Calah and Resen between Nineveh and Calah: this is the great city." According to this, Nimrod established the first Babylonian Empire.

8 It was at Babel (called Babylon by the Greek-speaking Jews) that the confusion of the language of mankind took place, when Jehovah God displayed his disapproval at the building of the city and of a false religious tower therein, because the builders purposed to make a celebrated name for themselves and to keep from being "scattered over all the surface of the earth." They did not foresee the decay of the cities that is taking place today. (Genesis 11:1-9) Though the first empire on earth, this Babylonian Empire of Nimrod did not become the First World Power of Bible record. Ancient Egypt did. Babel's political power was weakened, because its builders, now disunited by differing languages, were thus made by Jehovah to scatter over all the earth.

9 Jehovah God did not choose Babylon as the city on which to place his name. Noah and his blessed son Shem had no part in the building of Babel and its tower of false religion, and their language was not confused.

---

7. Which grandson of Ham established the first Babylonian Empire, and how?
8, 9. (a) Why did Jehovah not choose Babel as the city on which to place his name? (b) Whose language was not changed at Babel?

10 Two years after Noah's death in 2020 B.C.E., Abraham was born in the line of Shem, who was still alive. This descendant proved to be a worshiper of Shem's God, Jehovah. Shem could have had great satisfaction when he learned of the thrilling disclosure that Jehovah made to Abraham. This proved that Jehovah was sticking to his "eternal purpose" that He had formed at the garden of Eden after the transgression by Eve and Adam. It narrowed down the coming of the "seed" of God's "woman" to the line of Abraham, out of all the descendants of Shem. But what was the divine disclosure to Abraham, who at the time was called Abram?

11 Abram (Abraham) was in Mesopotamia, at the city of Ur of the Chaldeans not far from Babylon (Babel), when the disclosure was made to him. Genesis 12:1-3 tells us: "And Jehovah proceeded to say to Abram: 'Go your way out of your country and from your relatives and from the house of your father to the country that I shall show you; and I shall make a great nation out of you and I shall bless you and I will make your name great; and prove yourself a blessing. And I will bless those who bless you, and him that calls down evil upon you I shall curse, and all the families of the ground will certainly bless themselves by means of you.'"

12 "All the families of the ground"—that includes our families today in this twentieth century! Those of our families can procure a blessing by means of this ancient Abram (Abraham)! That is good news, indeed! And it broke upon the post-Deluge world of mankind away back there in the twentieth century before our Common Era. What this meant is commented on later in these inspired words: "Surely you know that those who adhere to faith are the ones who are sons of Abraham. Now the Scripture, seeing in advance that God would declare people of the nations righteous due to faith, declared the good news beforehand to Abraham, namely: 'By means of you all the nations will be blessed.'" (Galatians 3:7, 8) In

10, 11. (a) In Shem's days the line of descent for the promised "seed" was narrowed down to which of his descendants? (b) This was indicated by what disclosure, to whom?
12. For whom was that disclosure "good news," and what era may be said to have begun at that disclosure?

view of that it may rightly be said that the Era of the Good News (the Gospel Age, as some might want to call it) began back there shortly before Abraham obeyed the divine command.

¹³ A fact to be noted here, also, is that, at the time of God's choice of him to be the channel of blessing to all families and nations, Abraham was not circumcised in the flesh. God's command to him to get himself and his household males circumcised did not come till at least twenty-four years later, the year before the birth of his son Isaac (1918 B.C.E.). If not Abraham's fleshly condition, what was it, then, that counted with God? It was Abraham's faith. Jehovah God knew that Abraham had faith in Him. Not in vain did He issue to Abraham the command to leave his homeland. Abraham promptly left and moved with his household northwestward to Haran, and from there, after the death of his father Terah in Haran, he crossed the Euphrates River and moved toward the land that God was proceeding to show him. His crossing of the Euphrates River occurred on Nisan 14 in the spring of the year 1943 B.C.E., or 430 years before the celebration of the first Passover by Abraham's descendants down in Egypt.—Exodus 12:40-42; Galatians 3:17.

¹⁴ The prophet Moses made a record of this, writing: "At that Abram went just as Jehovah had spoken to him, and Lot went with him. And Abram was seventy-five years old when he went out from Haran. So Abram took Sarai his wife and Lot the son of his brother and all the goods that they had accumulated and the souls whom they had acquired in Haran, and they got on their way out to go to the land of Canaan. Finally they came to the land of Canaan. And Abram went on through the land as far as the site of Shechem, near the big trees of Moreh; and at that time the Canaanite was in the land. Jehovah now appeared to Abram and said: 'To your seed I am going to give this land.' After that he built an altar there to Jehovah, who had appeared to him."—Genesis 12:4-7; Acts 7:4, 5.

13. (a) What was the state of Abraham's flesh when God's command came to him, and so what was it that counted with God? (b) When did Abraham cross the Euphrates River?
14. What did Jehovah say to Abraham in the land of Canaan, and after that what did Abraham do?

¹⁵ Thus, although at that time Abram, at the age of seventy-five years, did not have any children, no child by his sixty-five-year-old wife Sarai, yet Jehovah promised that Abram would have a seed or offspring, to which Jehovah would give the land of Canaan. Abraham accepted that divine promise in faith. For, according to female powers of reproduction by that time back there, this approached onto God's promising a miracle. Twenty-four years later, when Abraham heard that he was to have a son by his wife Sarah he laughed and said in his heart: "Will a man a hundred years old have a child born, and will Sarah, yes, will a woman ninety years old give birth?" (Genesis 17:17; 18:12-14) If that was "extraordinary," still more marvelous would be the miracle that would fulfill God's prophecy in Genesis 3:15. This was because God's "woman" was heavenly and her promised "seed" would be heavenly and yet that "seed" would be tied in with Abraham's earthly line of descent. In this way this "seed" of God's "woman" could be called "the seed of Abraham," yes, "son of Abraham."

¹⁶ At the time that God, by his angel, assured Abraham that he was to have a son by his wife Sarah, to be named Isaac, God said to Abraham: "I will make you very, very fruitful and will make you become nations, and kings will come out of you. . . . I will bless her [Sarah] and also give you a son from her; and I will bless her and she shall become nations; kings of peoples will come from her." (Genesis 17:6, 16) So, now, which of those "nations" would be Jehovah's favored nation? Would it have a king over it? Would the "seed" of God's "woman" become that king? It is but natural to ask such questions.

MELCHIZEDEK

¹⁷ Before this, Abraham had had contact with earthly kings. The most significant of such contacts was when he met the outstanding king in the land of Canaan. Abraham had just been obliged to rescue his nephew

---

15. Why would God's promise of a "seed" to Abraham call for a miracle, this involving what still greater miracle?
16. God's promise to bring nations and kings out of Abraham and Sarah raised what questions regarding the "seed"?
17. What was the most outstanding contact with kings in Canaan-land in Abraham's career, and why did Abraham pay him a tithe?

Lot from the hands of four kings who had invaded the land of Canaan and defeated five of its kings and had carried off captives, including Lot. On his return from inflicting defeat upon those four marauder kings, Abraham approached the city of Salem, in the mountains to the west of the Dead Sea. "And Melchizedek king of Salem brought out bread and wine, and he was priest of the Most High God. Then he blessed him and said: 'Blessed be Abram of the Most High God, Producer of heaven and earth; and blessed be the Most High God, who has delivered your oppressors into your hand!' At that Abram gave him a tenth of everything." (Genesis 14:18-20) Since, as Melchizedek told Abraham, the Most High God had delivered Abraham's oppressors into his hand, it was only fitting that Abraham should give a tenth of all the spoils to the priest of the Most High God, Melchizedek.

[18] Melchizedek's blessing upon Abraham was not an empty utterance. It counted for something, and was in line with Jehovah's own promise that Abraham should be a blessing to all the families of the ground —all families should procure a blessing by means of him. (Genesis 12:3) This mysterious King-Priest Melchizedek, although given such scant mention in history, was not lost to sight. Nine hundred years later the Most High God inspired another king of Salem, King David of Jerusalem, to prophesy and show just how significant Melchizedek had been within the purpose of the Most High God. According to this, Melchizedek was the prefiguring of a still greater king, one even greater than David, one whom even David would be obliged to call "my Lord." This prefigured king could be no one else but the Messiah, the "seed" of God's "woman." So, under the power of God's holy spirit, David wrote, in Psalm 110:1-4:

"The utterance of Jehovah to my Lord is: 'Sit at my right hand until I place your enemies as a stool for your feet.' The rod of your strength Jehovah will send out of Zion, saying: 'Go subduing in the midst of your enemies.' Your people will offer themselves willingly on the day of your military force. In the splendors of holiness, from the womb of the dawn, you have your company of young men just like dewdrops. Jehovah has sworn (and he will feel no regret): 'You are a

18. Why was Melchizedek's blessing upon Abraham no empty utterance, and how did David show that one's importance in God's purpose?

priest to time indefinite according to the manner of Melchizedek!'"

19 Note what those inspired words signify. The fact that King David said that Jehovah would send out the King's rod of strength from Zion indicates that the King would be a fleshly descendant of David. According to Jehovah's covenant with David for an everlasting kingdom, no one would sit as king on Mount Zion and wield the rodlike scepter of strength except a fleshly descendant of David. (2 Samuel 7:8-16) Hence, this one whose rod of strength would be sent out of Zion would be called a "son of David." But in this case David was not referring prophetically to his son, King Solomon, who was the most glorious king of David's line to throne on Mount Zion and reign over all twelve tribes of his people. David never addressed his son Solomon as "My Lord," neither any other of the kings on Zion who followed Solomon all the way down to King Zedekiah. Furthermore, neither Solomon nor any of the succeeding kings on Mount Zion were priests as well as kings, as Melchizedek was.—2 Chronicles 26:16-23.

20 However, since this promised ruler was to be a "son" of King David, why would David refer to him as "My Lord"? This was due to the fact that this outstanding "son of David" would be a king far higher than David. Although David sat on the "throne of Jehovah" on earthly Mount Zion, he never, even at his death, ascended to heaven and sat down on the "right hand" of Jehovah. But the one who would become David's "Lord" would do so. His royal position at Jehovah's right hand in heaven could be referred to as a heavenly Mount Zion because it was pictured by the earthly Mount Zion, which used to be enclosed within Jerusalem's walls but is not so today. As Jehovah himself said, in Psalm 89:27, with regard to the Messiah: "Also, I myself shall place him as firstborn, the most high of the kings of the earth." Not alone would he be a lordly King higher than David, but he would also be forever a "priest" of the Most

---

19. The one prophesied to wield the rod of strength on Mount Zion had to be whose descendant, and why was David not prophesying about kings from Solomon to Zedekiah?
20. How would this prophetic one, although being David's son, yet be David's "Lord"?

High God, like Melchizedek the king of ancient Salem. —Psalm 76:2; 110:4.

21 Little did the patriarch Abraham, back there in the twentieth century B.C.E., realize that the "kings" to whom he and his wife Sarah were to become the ancestors would include the Messianic king who was foreshadowed by Melchizedek, to whom Abraham paid tithes of all his spoils of conquest. No wonder that Abraham's name was to become great because of its association with such a King-Priest! No wonder that, through this Priest-King like Melchizedek, all the families of the earth would bless themselves or procure a blessing by means of Abraham!—Genesis 12:3.

THE "FRIEND" OF GOD

22 After Abraham's victorious encounter with the four invading kings, God promised Abraham the needed protection and also that his "heir" would be a natural son of his. That God's chosen nation would come through this son and heir, God assured Abraham by means of an illustration: "He now brought him outside and said: 'Look up, please, to the heavens and count the stars, if you are possibly able to count them.' And he went on to say to him: 'So your seed will become.' And he put faith in Jehovah; and he proceeded to count it to him as righteousness."—Genesis 15:1-6.

23 Let us not forget that, at this time, Abraham was still an uncircumcised Hebrew. Hence, righteousness could not be counted to Abraham due to his being circumcised in the flesh; it was counted to him because of his faith in Jehovah, who was revealing part of his purpose to Abraham. So Abraham was counted righteous before God; he was thus justified to friendship with Jehovah God. Centuries later King Jehoshaphat of Jerusalem called Abraham the friend or "lover" of Jehovah. Still later, through the prophet Isaiah, Jehovah spoke of him as "Abraham my friend." (2 Chronicles 20:7; Isaiah 41:8) This proves how valuable, how vital, faith in Jehovah in connection with his "seed" really is.

21. Why, then, would Abraham's name become great?
22. How did God illustrate that His chosen nation would come through Abraham's natural son and heir?
23. On the basis of what was righteousness counted to Abraham, and to what was he justified?

²⁴ In the year 1932 B.C.E., at the suggestion of his barren, aged wife Sarah, Abraham had a son by means of her Egyptian slave girl Hagar and called him name Ishmael. (Genesis 16:1-16) Thirteen years thereafter, in 1919 B.C.E., Jehovah told Abraham that Ishmael was not to serve as the true "seed," but a son by his true wife Sarah would be the chosen "seed." It would be a son by a free woman. And so, in the succeeding year, Isaac was born when Sarah was ninety years of age. "And Abraham was a hundred years old when Isaac his son was born to him." On the eighth day of life Isaac was circumcised, just as his father Abraham had been just the year previous.—Genesis 21:1-5.

²⁵ It is interesting to note that God did not now make a nation out of his two sons, Ishmael the first-born and Isaac, a two-tribe nation. No, but five years later, at the urgent request of his wife Sarah, Abraham dismissed Hagar and her son Ishmael from his household, to fend for themselves, to go wherever they wanted to go. (Genesis 21:8-21) Neither afterward, after the death of Sarah in 1881 B.C.E., did God make a nation out of Isaac and the other sons that Abraham had by means of a concubine, Keturah, a seven-tribe nation. "Later on Abraham gave everything he had to Isaac, but to the sons of the concubines that Abraham had Abraham gave gifts. Then he sent them away from Isaac his son, while he was still alive, eastward, to the land of the East."—Genesis 25:1-6.

²⁶ A very admirable demonstration of faith on the part of Abraham led to a great blessing for this "friend" of Jehovah. It came after a penetrating test of Abraham's faith and obedience toward the Most High God. The blessing of divine approval was pronounced at a mountaintop in the land of Moriah, thought by many to be the location where King Solomon built the magnificent temple of Jehovah centuries afterward. (2 Chronicles 3:1) There, at the place designated by Jehovah, and on the wood spread out over a newly made stone altar, lay the form of

24. How did Abraham become father to Ishmael, and then how to Isaac?
25. What does the account show as to whether Jehovah made a nation including all the natural sons of Abraham?
26. For what admirable demonstration of faith did Abraham receive a special blessing in the land of Moriah, and what did it state?

a growing boy. It was Isaac. Beside the altar stood his father Abraham with a slaughtering knife in his hand. He was just about to carry out God's command to kill Isaac sacrificially and offer him up as a burnt offering to the God who had given him the boy miraculously. Then:

"Jehovah's angel began calling to him out of the heavens and saying: 'Abraham, Abraham!' . . . Do not put out your hand against the boy and do not do anything at all to him, for now I do know that you are God-fearing in that you have not withheld your son, your only one, from me.' . . . And Jehovah's angel proceeded to call to Abraham the second time out of the heavens and to say: 'By myself I do swear,' is the utterance of Jehovah, 'that by reason of the fact that you have done this thing and you have not withheld your son, your only one, I shall surely bless you and I shall surely multiply your seed like the stars of the heavens and like the grains of sand that are on the seashore; and your seed will take possession of the gate of his enemies. And by means of your seed all nations of the earth will certainly bless themselves due to the fact that you have listened to my voice.'"—Genesis 22:1-18.

27 This meant that the promised "seed" by means of whom all the nations would procure a blessing would come through Isaac's line of descent. Thereby Jehovah God showed that he was doing the choosing of the line of descent, and that all the half brothers of Isaac would have no part in furnishing that "seed." Nevertheless, the nations that descended from Isaac's half brothers could procure for themselves a blessing by means of that "seed." All nations of today, that is, people of all nationalities of today, can likewise procure a blessing through Abraham's "seed."

28 The patriarch Shem, a survivor of the global deluge, lived on to learn of that divine blessing pronounced upon Abraham; in fact, Shem lived on to learn of the marriage of Isaac to the beautiful Rebekah from Haran in Mesopotamia. Shem lived on to 1868 B.C.E., ten years after that marriage, but did not live to see the offspring of that marriage. But Abraham did so.—Genesis 11:11; 25:7.

---

27. What did this divine statement show as to the choosing of the "seed" and as to the procuring of the blessing through it?
28. Shem lived long enough to learn of what events in connection with his line of descent?

CHAPTER 8

The Divine Choosing According to the "Eternal Purpose"

JEHOVAH GOD chose to renew to Isaac the covenant promise made to his father Abraham. (Genesis 26:1-5, 23, 24) Although married at forty years of age, Isaac had to become sixty years old before he had children—twins. Would Jehovah, who answered Isaac's prayer for children, make a choosing with regard to those twin boys?

2 Jehovah indicated his choosing during Rebekah's pregnancy after she had prayed and asked him about her condition: "Jehovah proceeded to say to her: 'Two nations are in your belly, and two national groups will be separated from your inward parts; and the one national group will be stronger than the other national group, and the older will serve the younger.'" Esau proved to be the firstborn, and Jacob the second twin. (Genesis 25:20-23) Jehovah thus indicated that he would not make one nation out of these twin sons of Isaac, a two-tribe nation. Rather, there should be two national groups, with the national group from the older twin being weaker and serving the national group of the younger twin. This reversed the natural right of the firstborn son to the preeminence. Thus Jehovah revealed whom he would choose.

3 The Almighty, All-Wise God had a right to do this, according to his purpose for the blessing of all mankind. Regarding this, a first-century Bible commentator wrote: "When Rebekah conceived twins from the one man, Isaac our forefather: for when they had not yet been born nor had practiced anything good or vile,

1. What question arose as to the offspring of the man to whom God renewed his covenant promise?
2. How did Jehovah reveal which one of the twins he would choose?
3. Did the choosing there depend upon human works or upon the one who does the calling?

in order that the purpose of God respecting the choosing might continue dependent, not upon works, but upon the One who calls, it was said to her: 'The older will be the slave of the younger.' Just as it is written: 'I loved Jacob, but Esau I hated.' "—Romans 9:10-13; quoting also from Malachi 1:2, 3.

⁴ Certainly the Almighty, All-Wise God did not make a bad choice. Doubtless He, being able to read the genetic pattern of the twins in Rebekah's womb, foresaw how the two boys would work out the direction of their lives. So He chose the right twin, even though this one happened to be the younger twin. Despite his choice according to his purpose, Jehovah did not force matters. He did not plan for the older Esau to sell his birthright for a mere bowl of lentil stew to his younger brother Jacob on a critical day of decision. Evidently, however, Jehovah foresaw that the unborn Esau would not have the appreciation and love for spiritual things such as Jacob would have. For this reason he had less love for Esau than for Jacob and made his choice accordingly, even while the twins were yet unborn in their mother's womb.—Genesis 25:24-34.

⁵ Jehovah did not plan the tactics that Jacob and his mother Rebekah used finally with regard to getting the spoken blessing through Isaac, but Jehovah permitted the aged blind Isaac to pronounce the birthright blessing upon Jacob, as Jacob deserved to get it. (Genesis 27:1-30) Jehovah did not let Isaac reverse that blessing, but, when Jacob was fleeing from the murderous wrath of his twin brother Esau, God confirmed Isaac's blessing upon Jacob. This upheld God's choice of Jacob before his birth. How so?

⁶ At the place called Bethel in the Promised Land, the fugitive Jacob "began to dream, and, look! there was a ladder stationed upon the earth and its top reaching up to the heavens; and, look! there were God's angels ascending and descending on it. And, look! there was Jehovah stationed above it, and he proceeded to say: 'I am Jehovah the God of Abraham your father

---

4. Why did Jehovah have less love for Esau than for Jacob, even before their birth?
5. Did Jehovah plan how Jacob should get the spoken blessing of Isaac, and did He reverse it?
6. How was God's choice of Jacob upheld in the dream that Jacob had of the ladder used by angels?

and the God of Isaac. The land upon which you are lying, to you I am going to give it and to your seed. And your seed will certainly become like the dust particles of the earth, and you will certainly spread abroad to the west and to the east and to the north and to the south, and by means of you and by means of your seed all the families of the ground will certainly bless themselves. And here I am with you and I will keep you in all the way you are going and I will return you to this ground, because I am not going to leave you until I have actually done what I have spoken to you.'"—Genesis 28:12-15.

[7] According to this irreversible statement of the God who does not lie, the Abrahamic Promise set forth in Genesis 12:1-7 was to be carried out by God through Jacob's descendants or seed.

[8] This meant that the Messiah, the "seed" of God's heavenly "woman," was to come through Jacob's line of descent. That is why we specialize on following the history of Jacob's descendants rather than on the history of the nations and the families of the ground who are yet to be blessed by the Messianic "seed." Also, the God of Abraham and Isaac came to be called the "God of Jacob." This cannot be said for Esau (or, Edom), who did not distinguish himself in the worship of Jehovah and whose descendants became enemies of the worshipers of Jehovah. The idol Qos was the 'god of Edom.' (2 Chronicles 25:14; Ezekiel, chapter thirty-five) The temple built later on at Jerusalem came to be called "the house of the God of Jacob." (Isaiah 2:3) As an example for us now in these troublous days, the inspired psalmist says: "Jehovah of armies is with us; the God of Jacob is a secure height for us."—Psalm 46:11.

CHOICE OF THE ROYAL TRIBE

[9] While away for twenty years in Paddan-aram in the Mesopotamian valley, Jacob married into the family relationship approved by his father Isaac and became the father of eleven sons. Then God told him to

---

7, 8. (a) This divine statement meant what for Messiah's line of descent? (b) Unlike Esau, Jacob distinguished himself for whose worship?
9. (a) Why are Jacob's descendants called Israelites? (b) At what place did Jacob become father to his twelfth son?

return to the Promised Land, from which he had fled. (Genesis 31:3) It was while Jacob was on his return journey that he was given the surname Israel. God's angel said to him: "Your name will no longer be called Jacob but Israel, for you have contended with God and with men so that you at last prevailed." (Genesis 32:28) Thereafter Jacob's descendants were called Israelites. (Exodus 17:11) Later, when Jacob or Israel was on his way back from a revisit to Bethel, where he had had the ladder dream, he became father to his twelfth son, Benjamin. But at the delivery of this her second son, Jacob's beloved wife Rachel died. As recorded at Genesis 35:19, "thus Rachel died and was buried on the way to Ephrath, that is to say, Bethlehem."

10 After Jacob's return to the Promised Land in 1761 B.C.E., he continued living there as an alien resident for thirty-three years. During that time a number of significant things happened, but not according to any plan by God. Jacob's father, Isaac, died at the age of one hundred and eighty years. (Genesis 35:27-29) Jacob's oldest son, Reuben, sexually violated his father's concubine, Bilhah the maidservant of Rachel. (Genesis 35:22) This disqualified Reuben from enjoying the right of firstborn to his father Jacob and also from having the royal Messiah come through his line of descent. This certainly was not planned by Jehovah God, for He is no party to such incestuous fornication. —Genesis 49:1-4.

11 Prior to Rachel's death and to Reuben's act of shocking immorality, Jacob's daughter Dinah was sexually violated by an inhabitant of the Promised Land, namely, Shechem the son of Hamor the Hivite, who lived in the city of Shechem. There was great indignation among Jacob's sons because of this "disgraceful folly against Israel." So, when the male inhabitants of Shechem were incapacitated because of their compliance with the requirement of circumcision, Jacob's second son Simeon and his third son Levi took swords and massacred all such unsuspecting male Shechemites, after which the city was plundered.

10. During Jacob's further stay in the Promised Land, what disqualifications did Reuben come under?
11, 12. (a) How did Simeon and Levi disqualify themselves from any opportunity as to the Messianic line? (b) What must God now do as to the choosing?

¹² Jacob as God's prophet disapproved of this violence. He told Simeon and Levi that they had thereby made him a "stench to the inhabitants of the land" and had exposed him and his household to annihilation by the more numerous peoples of the land. (Genesis 34:1-30) Because of such cruel slaughter in anger and fury, Simeon and Levi disqualified themselves of either one of them having his line of descent lead down to the Messianic "seed." So this honorable privilege must now go to some other son aside from Simeon and Levi and the natural firstborn son Reuben. (Genesis 49:5-7) Certainly Jehovah God had not planned matters that way. He now had to adapt himself to the new set of circumstances. His choice among the yet remaining sons of Jacob He would yet indicate by means of his prophet, Jacob or Israel.

¹³ The firstborn son of Jacob's beloved second wife, Rachel, was the eleventh son of the family, namely, Joseph. Jacob displayed special affection for this son of his old age. For this reason Joseph's half brothers became jealous of him. Without the knowledge of their father, they managed to sell Joseph to traveling merchants who were on their way down to Egypt. They led Jacob their father to believe that Joseph had been killed by a wild beast.

¹⁴ Joseph was sold into slavery in Egypt, but by the favor of the God whom he faithfully worshiped and obeyed he was raised to be food administrator and prime minister of Egypt under Pharaoh. In the year 1728 B.C.E. Joseph became reconciled with his repentant half brothers, who had come down to Egypt for food supplies during the world famine. Thereafter, by Joseph's arrangements, his father Jacob or Israel moved with all his household down to Egypt and settled in what was called the Land of Goshen. There Jacob continued to live for seventeen years.—Genesis, chapters 37-47.

¹⁵ It was at God's instructions that Jacob left the Promised Land and went down to Egypt at Joseph's invitation. (Genesis 46:1-4) He went down there as still the heir of the Abrahamic Promise and the one

---

13, 14. How did Jacob and his household come to move down into Egypt to be with Joseph there?
15, 16. Jacob then entered Egypt as still heir of what, and how is this called to attention in Psalm 105:7-15?

to pass it on. Psalm 105:7-15 points to this fact and says:

16 "He is Jehovah our God. His judicial decisions are in all the earth. He has remembered his covenant even to time indefinite, the word that he commanded, to a thousand generations, which covenant he concluded with Abraham, and his sworn statement to Isaac, and which statement he kept standing as a regulation even to Jacob, as an indefinitely lasting covenant even to Israel, saying: 'To you I shall give the land of Canaan as the allotment of your inheritance.' This was when they happened to be few in number, yes, very few, and alien residents in it. And they kept walking about from nation to nation, from one kingdom to another people. He did not allow any human to defraud them, but on their account he reproved kings, saying: 'Do not you men touch my anointed ones [in Hebrew the plural number of *ma·shi'ahh*, or messiahs], and to my prophets do nothing bad.' "—*Marginal reading*.

17 Thus Jehovah called Abraham, Isaac and Jacob his prophets, and this they really were. (Genesis 20:7) A prophet could be spoken of as being anointed because of being designated and appointed, even without the pouring of official oil upon him. (1 Kings 19:16, 19; 2 Kings 2:14) Likewise, although Abraham, Isaac and Jacob were not anointed with oil in the way that Jacob anointed the pillar at the place called Bethel, they were properly called "anointed ones" because of Jehovah's action toward them. (Genesis 28:18, 19; 31:13) The fact that Jehovah called them "my anointed ones" indicates that he appointed them, he chose them. Moffatt's Bible translation renders Psalm 105:15: "Never touch my chosen, never harm my prophets." (Also 1 Chronicles 16:22) Jehovah chooses whom he wants to; there is a purpose behind his choice.

18 Abraham, Isaac and Jacob were Jehovah's "messiahs," and it is in harmony with this that the Messianic nation came through them. The Holy Scriptures speak of this chosen nation as Jehovah's "messiah" or "anointed one." In Psalm 28:8, 9, the psalmist

17. Why did Jehovah speak of Abraham, Isaac and Jacob as being "prophets" and as being his "anointed ones"?
18. Accordingly, the nation that was to come through Abraham, Isaac and Jacob was also how designated, and why appropriately so?

David says: "Jehovah is a strength to his people, and he is a stronghold of the grand salvation of his anointed one [Hebrew: *ma·shi'ahh*]. Do save your people, and bless your inheritance; and shepherd them and carry them to time indefinite." Later, the prophet Habakkuk said to Jehovah in prayer: "You went forth for the salvation of your people, to save your anointed one [*ma·shi'ahh*]." (Habakkuk 3:13) It was in line with this that, through this "anointed" people or nation, there was to come in God's appointed time the real Messiah, the "seed" of God's heavenly "woman." —Genesis 3:15.

19 It was down in Egypt that Jacob's descendants grew to be a numerous people, ready for nationhood. It was concerning the time that Jacob was on his deathbed (in 1711 B.C.E.) and gave his farewell words to his sons that it was said: "All these are the twelve tribes of Israel, and this is what their father spoke to them when he was blessing them. He blessed them each one according to his own blessing." (Genesis 49:28) By becoming each one the head of a tribe, these twelve sons of Jacob were called "patriarchs," or 'heads of the fathers.' As a speaker before the Jerusalem Sanhedrin once said: "He then gave him the covenant of circumcision, and so, after Isaac was born, he circumcised him on the eighth day; and Isaac begot Jacob, and Jacob the twelve patriarchs. The patriarchs out of jealousy sold Joseph into slavery in Egypt, but God was with him." (Acts 7:8, 9, *New English Bible*) Properly, the Greek-speaking Jews spoke of "Abraham the patriarch," and also of "the patriarch David." —Hebrews 7:4; Acts 2:29, *NEB*.

20 This does not mean, however, that a religious patriarchate was set up among Jacob's descendants there in Egypt. After Jacob's death in the land of Goshen, Joseph as the prime minister of Egypt for Pharaoh did not set himself up as the patriarchal head of the "twelve tribes of Israel," even though his father's final blessing upon him indicated that the right of firstborn had been transferred to Joseph.—Genesis 49:22-26; 50:15-26.

---

19. Being heads of twelve tribes, the sons of Jacob were called what?
20. Was a religious patriarchate thus set up in Israel?

²¹ By his prophetic blessings upon his twelve sons the patriarch Jacob disclosed more than that the birthright or right of the firstborn had been transferred from Reuben, Jacob's firstborn son by his first wife Leah, to Joseph, the firstborn son of his second wife Rachel. (Genesis 29:21-32) Before selling Joseph into slavery in Egypt, his half brothers resented the thought that he might become king over them. (Genesis 37:8) But long previous to this, when God gave to the patriarch Abraham the covenant of circumcision, God foretold that kings would come out of Abraham, and this by means of his wife Sarah, whose name God then changed from Sarai to Sarah, meaning "Princess." (Genesis 17:16) Also, when God changed Jacob's name to Israel, he promised that kings would come out of Jacob. (Genesis 35:10, 11) However, the right of the firstborn son of the family did not automatically carry with it the right and honor to be the ancestor to the line of kings that would lead up to the Messianic King, the "seed" of God's heavenly "woman." This vital matter depended upon God's choice. He caused Jacob to point out which son would be ancestor to such King.

²² After expressing his disapproval of Reuben, Simeon and Levi, the dying Jacob said with reference to his fourth son by his first wife Leah: "As for you, Judah, your brothers will laud you. Your hand will be on the back of the neck of your enemies. The sons of your father will prostrate themselves to you. A lion cub Judah is. From the prey, my son, you will certainly go up. He bowed down, he stretched himself out like a lion and, like a lion, who dares rouse him? The scepter will not turn aside from Judah, neither the commander's staff from between his feet, until Shiloh comes; and to him the obedience of the peoples will belong."—Genesis 49:8-10.

²³ Let us note Jacob's comparison of Judah with a lion. Micah 5:8 likens a lion to an animal king of the forest. Ezekiel 19:1-9 likens the kings of the kingdom

---

21. (a) Jacob indicated that the right of firstborn was now transferred to whom? (b) Choice of the head one of the line leading to the Messianic king depended upon whom?
22. In a blessing, over which son did Jacob refer to a "scepter" and a "commander's staff"?
23. All those features, scepter, commander's staff, obedience of the peoples, comparison with a lion, bespeak what for Judah?

of Judah to lions. So Jacob's comparison of Judah with a lion goes well with the fact that the scepter was not to "turn aside from Judah," this implying that Judah already had the scepter and would not lose it or be deprived of it. That this was the scepter of kingship is bolstered up by the fact that the scepter was linked with the "commander's staff," which also was not to turn away from Judah before Shiloh would come. Furthermore, to Judah, as represented by this Shiloh, "the obedience of the peoples will belong." (Genesis 49:10) All these features about Judah bespeak royalty!

24 The name Shiloh is understood to mean "The One Whose It Is." The ancient Latin *Vulgate,* which was translated from the original Hebrew text of the day, reads: "Until he comes who is to be sent."

25 The coming of this Shiloh ("The One Whose It Is") refers to the same one whose coming is foretold in the words of the Sovereign Lord Jehovah to the last Judean king of Jerusalem: "A ruin, a ruin, a ruin I shall make it. As for this also, it will certainly become no one's until he comes who has the legal right, and I must give it to him." (Ezekiel 21:27) This undoubtedly refers to the coming of the Messianic King, the "seed" of God's figurative "woman," for with his coming there is no need of a further succession of kings after him. Then the kingdom in the tribe of Judah reaches its culmination and remains forever in the hands of Shiloh. This is the Messianic King that will sit at Jehovah's right hand in the heavens and will be a king like Melchizedek, to whom the patriarch Abraham paid the tithes of the spoils of victory. (Psalm 110:1-4) Thus the royal scepter would not turn aside from Judah.

26 That the right of the firstborn son of the family was one thing and the assignment of royal leadership was another thing, and that God through the dying patriarch Jacob assigned the royal leadership to Judah, is plainly stated in Scripture. In 1 Chronicles 5:1, 2 we read concerning the sons of Jacob: "And the sons of Reuben the firstborn of Israel—for he was the first-

---

24, 25. (a) What does the name Shiloh mean, and to whom does it apply? (b) Why will the royal scepter not have to turn aside from Judah?
26. (a) How does 1 Chronicles 5:1, 2 show right of firstborn to be one thing and royal connections another? (b) Despite unplanned developments, Jehovah was free and able to do what?

born; but for his profaning the lounge of his father his right as firstborn was given to the sons of Joseph the son of Israel, so that he [Reuben] was not to be enrolled genealogically for the right of the firstborn. For Judah himself proved to be superior among his brothers, and the one for leader was from him [and the prince descended from him (*Leeser*); and of him came he that is the prince (*Jewish Publication Society*)]; but the right as firstborn was Joseph's." We cannot here say that the Almighty, All-Wise God planned it this way, for he did not induce the misdeeds of Reuben, Simeon and Levi and the consequences thereof. Rather, according to the way that the unplanned developments worked out he was free to make choice of Judah. Regardless of what happened he was able to stick to his original purpose and to work it out without change.

27 God's choices and movements serve as a sure guide for us as we consider His "eternal purpose" that he formed in connection with the Anointed One, the Messiah. From the prophetic words that he inspired the dying patriarch Jacob to pronounce over Judah, we know the course for us to follow. We must keep our eyes trained, not merely upon the twelve tribes of Israel in general, but upon the tribe of Judah in particular because of its direct relationship with Jehovah's Messiah, the "seed" of His heavenly "woman." More and more evidence is accumulating to aid us to identify this Messianic King with whom God's "eternal purpose" is wrapped up.

28 Acting upon the evidence as the Sovereign Lord Jehovah furnishes it to us, we shall avoid becoming followers of a disappointing false Messiah. We shall, instead, experience the joy of recognizing the true Messiah from God and following the one by means of whom all the nations of the earth will procure an eternal blessing.

27, 28. (a) Upon what nation, then, shall we keep our eyes trained, and upon which part thereof in particular? (b) By acting upon the evidence that God furnishes, what benefits shall we enjoy?

CHAPTER 9

A Nation That Entered a Covenant with God

IN INTERNATIONAL affairs it is customary for one state to enter a treaty with another state for mutual defense or peaceful relations or cultural exchanges or other considerations. A number of political states may enter an organization under a treaty, such as, today, the North Atlantic Treaty Organization (NATO), the Warsaw Treaty Organization (or, Warsaw Pact), or the Southeast Asia Treaty Organization (SEATO). But what political state or nation today is in a covenant with God? Nations today are too materialistic to form a treaty organization with an invisible heavenly Being as a party to the treaty.

2 Anciently, however, there was a real, live nation on earth that entered a covenant with the Most High God of heaven. This meant a covenant between an earthly party and a heavenly party, a visible party and an invisible party. Every covenant has a stated purpose. What was the purpose of that historic covenant between a nation on earth and the one living and true God in heaven? How was such a seemingly unbalanced covenant made? These are questions that we now want to get answered.

3 Being all-wise and all-powerful, the Most High God would be the proper One to offer or even to propose such a covenant with a nation of imperfect, sinful people. Under the circumstances, it would be fitting for Him to state the purpose of the covenant and to dictate its terms and to appoint a mediator to act between Him and men. He would set forth the conditions on which the covenant would continue and also choose the time for establishing such a covenant or compact. The time fixed by God long beforehand was

1. Nations today are too materialistic to form a treaty organization with whom?
2. What questions do we want answered about a nation that entered a covenant with God?
3. Who would be the proper one to arrange for the terms, mediator, conditions and time of such a covenant?

in the sixteenth century before our Common Era (or B.C.E.).

⁴ God had made a formal covenant over sacrifice with the forefather of this whole nation that was to be taken into a national covenant in due time. It was after Melchizedek, king of Salem and priest of the Most High God, pronounced a blessing upon the militarily victorious Abraham that God brought Abraham into this formal covenant with Him over sacrifice. When giving Abraham strong assurance that the divine promise would be fulfilled upon Abraham's descendants, God said to him: "You may know for sure that your seed will become an alien resident in a land not theirs, and they will have to serve them, and these will certainly afflict them for four hundred years. But the nation that they will serve I am judging, and after that they will go out with many goods. As for you, you will go to your forefathers in peace; you will be buried at a good old age. But in the fourth generation they will return here, because the error of the Amorites has not yet come to completion."—Genesis 15:13-16.

⁵ Thus the taking over of the land by the natural seed of Abraham was put off for more than four hundred years. This long period of time would allow for the chosen natural seed of Abraham to grow to a people of many members, numerous enough to displace the Amorite occupants of Canaanland who were going from bad to worse in the "error" of their pagan ways. Although Abraham's natural seed would grow to a people of great size in a land foreign to Canaanland, yet God would hold the land in reserve for them until the "error" of the promised land's inhabitants had become so bad that they deserved to be purged out of the land. That God would give the territory to Abraham's natural seed at the time ripe for it, Jehovah now guaranteed with a formal covenant.

"On that day Jehovah concluded with Abram a covenant, saying: 'To your seed I will give this land, from the river of Egypt to the great river, the river Euphrates: the Kenites and the Kenizzites and the Kadmonites and the Hittites and the Perizzites and the Rephaim and the Amorites and the Canaanites and the Girgashites and the Jebusites.' "—Genesis 15:18-21.

4. On the occasion of making a formal covenant with Abraham over sacrifice, what time period did God foretell for his seed?
5. The long time that was to pass before Abraham's seed would occupy the Promised Land allowed for what to take place?

⁶ In contrast with that divine covenant with but one man, Abraham, the covenant that God had in view was to be with a great nation of descendants from Abraham through the chosen line of descent. That national covenant was to be added to the Abrahamic Promise, which became binding when Abraham crossed the Euphrates River to the north and entered the territory that was included within the boundaries stated in God's formal covenant with Abraham over sacrifice. (Genesis 12:1-7) The making of the covenant with the nation of Abraham's descendants did not cancel out the Abrahamic Promise but was merely added to it. Wisely so, for not all the fleshly descendants of Abraham would prove suitable to share in the Abrahamic Promise as regards its fulfillment for the blessing of all the nations and families of the ground. Hence, the added national covenant would serve well as an aid or means to prepare the worthy ones to receive and loyally follow the true Messiah, the promised "seed" of God's heavenly "woman," when God sent and anointed this one.

⁷ The making of that additional national covenant would not take place before the passing of *more* than four hundred years from when God concluded this covenant with Abraham over sacrifice, because at that time Abraham did not have any offspring at all by his then barren wife, Sarah. Furthermore, God would not make a covenant with Abraham's descendants when they were in servitude and being afflicted by a foreign nation. Especially so, when the making of the covenant called for that type of sacrifices that were detestable and objectionable to the nation afflicting them and enslaving them. (Exodus 8:25-27) First after God had judged adversely the oppressive nation and delivered his people and made them free to undertake a covenant with Him would God establish a covenant with them. This would be at the end of the foretold "four hundred years." Thus we note that Jehovah God has marked off his own periods of time for the working

6. Would the national covenant cancel out the Abrahamic Promise, and what purpose would it serve as regards Abraham's descendants?
7. For what reasons would God not conclude the covenant with Abraham's descendants before the end of those four hundred years?

out of his "eternal purpose" in connection with his Anointed One, Messiah.

8 Twenty-five years after Abraham entered the Promised Land, or at the age of one hundred years, he became father to his one and only son by his true wife, Sarah, this being, of course, by a divine miracle. This was in the land that did not yet belong to Abraham or to his son Isaac. It was when Isaac was weaned that affliction began upon the natural "seed" through whom the Messiah was to come. This was when Isaac's nineteen-year-old half-brother Ishmael disrespectfully poked fun at the newly weaned Isaac. Such conduct showing jealousy could develop into a threat to the life of Abraham's God-given heir, Isaac.—Genesis 16:11, 12.

9 According to time measurements, this beginning of the afflicting of the "seed" of Abraham in a land that was not theirs occurred when Abraham was one hundred and five years old and Isaac was five years old. That was in the year 1913 B.C.E. (Genesis 21:1-9; Galatians 4:29) Accordingly, the "four hundred years" of affliction upon the natural "seed" of Abraham would end in 1513 B.C.E. That would be the year for Abraham's seed to go out from the land of the oppressive nation and start to return to the land of its forefathers, the Promised Land. That was the due time for God to establish the national covenant with Abraham's "seed," that he might bring them into the Promised Land as a nation in a binding covenant with Him. The time for this, at the end of the four hundred years, was also four hundred and thirty years after Abraham crossed the Euphrates River and the Abrahamic Promise took effect.—Exodus 12:40-42; Galatians 3:17-19.

ESTABLISHMENT OF A NATIONAL COVENANT

10 From when Abraham's grandson Jacob moved with his household out of the land of Canaan, and down to the end of the four hundred years, Jacob's descendants, the twelve tribes of Israel, found themselves in the land of Hamitic Egypt (not Arabic Egypt, as of today).

8, 9. (a) What time period began at the weaning of Isaac, and how so? (b) The end of that time period was the time for what regarding Abraham's natural seed?
10. To what extent did Abraham's natural seed grow in Egypt, but finally under what condition?

As foretold by Jehovah God, affliction had come upon Abraham's natural "seed" and had now grown very severe. The objective of this was to exterminate the people of God's friend, Abraham. In spite of this, they had increased to become like the stars of the heavens and like the grains of sand on the seashore, innumerable, as God had promised. Finally, they were able to muster up "six hundred thousand able-bodied men on foot," fit for military service. (Exodus 12:37) No, God had not forgotten his covenant with his friend Abraham. He also kept to his announced time schedule. So He was ready for due action at the due time.

11 Who should now be their visible leader? God did not choose the chieftain of the tribe of Judah as if that were obligatory because of the Kingdom blessing that Jacob had pronounced upon Judah. (Genesis 49:10; 1 Chronicles 5:1, 2) Instead, the Most High God, with his inherent right of choice, selected a fit man of the tribe of Levi, Moses the great-grandson of Levi. (Exodus 6:20; Numbers 26:58, 59) Forty years prior to the end of the four hundred years, Moses decided against the court life of Pharaoh of Egypt and threw in his lot with his Israelite brothers and offered himself to them as their leader to lead them out of slavery. "He was supposing his brothers would grasp that God was giving them salvation by his hand, but they did not grasp it." God had *then* not sent Moses to deliver the enslaved people. Moses was obliged to flee from Pharaoh's effort to kill him. He took refuge in the land of Midian and married and became a shepherd for his father-in-law.—Exodus 2:11 through 3:1; Acts 7:23-29.

12 Forty years passed, and Moses became eighty years of age. Then while Moses was shepherding on the Sinai Peninsula, God's angel made a miraculous manifestation to Moses at the foot of Mount Horeb, about two hundred miles southeast of the present-day Suez Canal. Here, at Horeb, Jehovah God spelled out his name, as it were, to Moses, saying: " 'I Shall Prove To Be What I Shall Prove To Be.' . . . This is what you are to say to the sons of Israel, 'I Shall Prove To Be

11. Whom did God raise up to be a leader for Israel, and how had this one tried to show himself a leader?
12. When and where did Moses become Jehovah's "anointed one," and with what mission?

has sent me to you.'" (Exodus 3:2-14) Thus God appointed Moses as His prophet and representative, and Moses could now correctly be called an "anointed one," or "messiah," the same as his forefathers Abraham, Isaac and Jacob. (Psalm 105:15; Acts 7:30-35; Hebrews 11:23-26) Jehovah indicated that Mount Horeb was where He would bring Moses' people into a covenant with Him, for Jehovah said that Moses would bring them out of Egypt to this mountain, there to serve Him.—Exodus 3:12.

13 Because of Pharaoh's repeated refusals to let the Israelites go free, Jehovah brought a series of plagues upon him and his people. The tenth and last plague was the one that broke the stout heart of Pharaoh and his resistance. This plague laid low in death all the firstborn ones of the Egyptian families and of their domestic animals. The Israelites were spared from the death of their firstborn because they obeyed Jehovah God and celebrated the Passover meal, their first one, in their homes. Jehovah's angel of judgment, beholding the blood of the Passover lamb splashed on the doorposts and upper crossbeam of their homes, passed them by, and death did not invade the family circle. Nahshon, the father of Salmon, of the tribe of Judah, was spared alive, also Nadab, the firstborn son of Moses' older brother, Aaron. But Pharaoh's firstborn son died. In grief and under insistence by the bereaved Egyptians, Pharaoh ordered the unharmed Israelites out of the country.—Exodus 5:1 to 12:51.

14 That eventful Passover night of the year 1513 B.C.E. brought to an end simultaneously a number of marked periods of time. The four hundred years of the afflicting of Abraham's natural seed in a land not theirs ended. Two hundred and fifteen years of residence in Egypt from the entry of the patriarch Jacob ended. Four hundred and thirty years counted from when Abraham crossed the Euphrates River and began dwelling in the Promised Land ended. No wonder we read: "And the dwelling of the sons of Israel, who had dwelt in Egypt, was four hundred and thirty years. And it came about at the end of the four hundred and

---

13. How was Pharaoh brought to the point of ordering the Israelites to leave Egypt?
14. What time periods ended on that first Passover day, and what did God order with respect to that night?

thirty years, it even came about on this very day that all the armies of Jehovah went out of the land of Egypt. It is a night for observance with regard to Jehovah for bringing them out of the land of Egypt. With regard to Jehovah this night is one for observance on the part of all the sons of Israel throughout their generations."—Exodus 12:40-42.

[15] As a piece of strategy, Jehovah by means of Moses led his liberated people to the shore of the upper western arm of the Red Sea. Imagining that the Israelites were trapped, Pharaoh and his charioteers and horsemen went in pursuit and closed in upon their escaped slaves. But Almighty God caused a passageway to open up and during the night the Israelites went through the dried seabed to the shores of the Sinai Peninsula. When the Egyptians were permitted to drive into the escape corridor, God brought back the waters of the Red Sea upon them and drowned them and their horses. God's word had not failed, that He would judge that nation of oppressors of the natural "seed" of Abraham. (Genesis 15:13, 14) Safe on Sinai's shores, the witnesses of the judgment of Jehovah sang: "Jehovah will rule as king to time indefinite, even forever. . . . Sing to Jehovah, for he has become highly exalted. The horse and its rider he has pitched into the sea."—Exodus 15:1-21.

[16] It marked a special day when the Israelites came, in the third lunar month (Sivan) after leaving Egypt, into the wilderness of Sinai and encamped at the base of the "mountain of the true God," Horeb. That is where Jehovah told Moses that they were to serve him. (Exodus 3:1, 12; 19:1) The prophet Moses was now called upon to act as the mediator between God and the encamped people. Jehovah now proposed a covenant between Himself and the people and set forth the purpose of the covenant. To Moses, up on Mount Horeb, He said: "This is what you are to say to the house of Jacob and to tell the sons of Israel, 'You yourselves have seen what I did to the Egyptians, that I might carry you on wings of eagles and bring you to myself. And now if you will strictly obey my voice

15. How did God deliver the Israelites from the pursuing Egyptians, and what did they then sing?
16. What did God propose to encamped Israel at Horeb, and what was the purpose thereof?

and will indeed keep my covenant, then you will certainly become my special property out of all other peoples, because the whole earth belongs to me. And you yourselves will become to me a kingdom of priests and a holy nation.'"—Exodus 19:3-6.

¹⁷ The Most High God did not force this covenant upon the Israelites. He left them free to choose whether to enter a covenant with him or not, even though he had saved them from Egypt and the Red Sea. Become a "special property" to Jehovah? Become "a kingdom of priests and a holy nation" to Him? Yes, that is what the Israelites then desired to do. Hence, when Moses told the representative men of the people about God's proposed covenant, then, as we read, "all the people answered unanimously and said: 'All that Jehovah has spoken we are willing to do.'" Moses now reported the decision of the people to Jehovah, who then proceeded with the establishing of the covenant as agreed to.—Exodus 19:7-9.

¹⁸ On the third day after that Jehovah, by means of his angel on Mount Sinai there in Horeb, declared to the assembled Israelites the Ten Words or Ten Commandments. These commandments we can read for ourselves in Exodus 20:2-17.

A GREATER MEDIATOR FORETOLD

¹⁹ The occasion was a spectacular one! "Now all the people were seeing the thunders and the lightning flashes and the sound of the horn and the mountain smoking. When the people got to see it, then they quivered and stood at a distance. And they began to say to Moses: 'You speak with us, and let us listen; but let not God speak with us for fear we may die.'" (Exodus 20:18, 19) The response of God in compliance with this request of the frightened Israelites is set out more fully in Deuteronomy 18:14-19. There, after telling the Israelites that God had not given them magicians and diviners as go-betweens between Him and them, Moses continued on to say:

---

17. What procedure shows whether Jehovah forced the covenant upon the saved Israelites?
18. On the third day therefrom, what did God declare to Israel?
19. (a) Because of the spectacle, what did the Israelites request of Moses? (b) What did Moses say in response?

"But as for you, Jehovah your God has not given you anything like this. A prophet from your own midst, from your brothers, like me, is what Jehovah your God will raise up for you—to him you people should listen—in response to all that you asked of Jehovah your God in Horeb on the day of the congregation, saying, 'Do not let me hear again the voice of Jehovah my God, and this great fire do not let me see anymore, that I may not die.' At that Jehovah said to me, 'They have done well in speaking what they did. A prophet I shall raise up for them from the midst of their brothers, like you; and I shall indeed put my words in his mouth, and he will certainly speak to them all that I shall command him. And it must occur that the man who will not listen to my words that he will speak in my name, I shall myself require an account from him.'"

20 A prophet like Moses, with whom God spoke, as it were "face to face"? It may have been hard for the Israelites to accept such an idea, when Moses himself told them what God had said. Yet, that is what Almighty God said that he would raise up for his people. 'Like Moses' would not mean merely equal to Moses. The promised prophet could be like Moses, and yet be greater than Moses.

21 From the Israelite prophets after Moses and all the way down to Malachi there was no prophet like Moses and none greater than Moses. (Deuteronomy 34:1-12) But what about the promised Anointed One, the Messiah, who would be the "seed" of God's heavenly "woman"? (Genesis 3:15) God was evidently speaking about this one when, at Mount Sinai, he spoke to Moses about a future prophet *like* Moses. Like Moses, this Messianic "seed" would be a Mediator between God and men, but greater than Moses. Certainly the worshipers of the one living and true God need to have more done for them now than was done for ancient Israel by Moses. So Moses prefigured the Greater Prophet of Jehovah who was to come.

22 At that time Jehovah God also said to Moses: "This is what you are to say to the sons of Israel, 'You yourselves have seen that it was from the heavens I spoke with you. You must not make along with me gods of silver, and you must not make gods of gold

20, 21. (a) Was it easy for Israel to believe there would be another prophet *like* Moses? (b) In what way was this future prophet to be like Moses, and on what scale?
22. Why would the coming prophet like Moses be against using images in worshiping God?

for yourselves.' " (Exodus 20:22, 23) Beyond all denial, this is a command against using lifeless, speechless, man-made images in the worship of the God who has spoken from heaven itself. It strongly emphasizes what God said in the second of the Ten Commandments, as stated in Exodus 20:4-6. The Messianic Prophet like Moses would be against such use of religious images.

23 Before the establishing of the covenant by means of his mediator Moses, God gave him other laws in addition to the Ten Commandments. These were set out in Exodus, chapters twenty-one through twenty-three. They were written down in a scroll or "book," which was on hand when the covenant was to be formally established. Since this covenant was specially marked by the giving of divine law for God's chosen people to keep, it was a covenant of law and is commonly called the Law Covenant. Its law code or set of laws in arranged form is Scripturally spoken of as "the Law."

24 Since the Law of this covenant with Israel was introduced in the form of the Ten Commandments just about fifty or fifty-one days after the Passover night in Egypt, it could properly be said that the Law "has come into being four hundred and thirty years later [after the Abrahamic covenant of 1943 B.C.E.]." The giving of the Law to Israel after such a long interval did not invalidate the Abrahamic covenant, "so as to abolish the promise." (Galatians 3:17) God's promise to bless all the nations and families of the ground in Abraham's "seed" still stands. It will not fail!

25 Let us be sure to note that the Law covenant with Israel was made valid, solemnly binding upon the parties to the covenant, by the applying of the blood of the sacrificial victims. The record in Exodus 24:6-8 tells us: "Then Moses [as the mediator] took half the blood and put it in bowls, and half the blood he sprinkled upon the altar. Finally he took the book of the covenant and read it in the ears of the people. Then they said: 'All that Jehovah has spoken we are

23. Why is that covenant with Israel commonly called the Law Covenant?
24. How long after the Abrahamic covenant was the Law covenant made, and is the Abrahamic Promise still valid?
25. Upon whom was the Law covenant made binding, and by the application of what to it?

willing to do and be obedient.' So Moses took the blood and sprinkled it upon the people and said: 'Here is the blood of the covenant that Jehovah has concluded with you as respects all these words.' "—Note also Exodus 24:3.

26 The altar that Moses had built at the base of Mount Sinai represented Jehovah God, to whom the sacrifices had been offered upon this altar. Hence, by the applying of half the blood of the animal victims to the altar, Jehovah God was representatively brought into the covenant and bound by it as a party to it. On the other hand, by the sprinkling of the other part of the sacrificial blood upon the people, they also were brought into the covenant as the other party thereto and were solemnly bound by it to fulfill those terms of it that applied to them. Thus by the blood the two parties, God and the nation of Israel, were united in a covenant.

27 The nation of Israel did not walk into this covenant ignorantly or under pressure and compulsion. The day before the solemnizing of the covenant with blood they had had God's words and decisions related to them and had accepted these. As Exodus 24:3 states: "Then Moses came and related to the people all the words of Jehovah and all the judicial decisions, and all the people answered with one voice and said: 'All the words that Jehovah has spoken we are willing to do.' " The following day, after Moses read the "book of the covenant" in the hearing of all the people, they repeated their acceptance of God's Law, after which they were sprinkled with the sacrificial blood. Now it was obligatory upon the whole nation of Israel to do what God had stated when proposing the covenant, saying: "Now if you will strictly obey my voice and will indeed keep my covenant, then . . . "—Exodus 19:5, 6.

28 Almighty God could be expected to be faithful to His part of this bilateral covenant, for He does not

---

26. What was represented by the applying of the blood to God's altar, and what by the sprinkling of the people with the blood?
27. What, in connection with the establishment of the Law covenant, proves that the Israelites did not walk into it ignorantly or under compulsion?
28. Which party to the Law covenant was put in question as to loyalty to its terms, and, to be holy, what was required?

change. (Malachi 3:6) It was the Israelites who were put in question. Would they be loyal to God in carrying out what they expressed willingness to do? Would they be among the loyal ones that were to be gathered to Jehovah, in fulfillment of Psalm 50:4, 5: "He calls to the heavens above and to the earth so as to execute judgment on his people: 'Gather to me my loyal ones, those concluding my covenant over sacrifice'"? (*NW; NEB*) Not as individuals, but as a whole people, as a nation, they had made this Law covenant over a set of sacrifices that were for all the people. Would they prove themselves to be "a holy nation"? To do this they must keep clear from this world.

²⁹ Just because of entering into this covenant with the Most High God they were not at once a "kingdom of priests." They were by no means then a kingdom in which every male member was a priest to God in behalf of all the other nations of the earth. The prophecy of Isaiah 61:6 was not yet fulfilled toward them: "As for you, the priests of Jehovah you will be called; the ministers of our God you will be said to be. The resources of the nations you people will eat, and in their glory you will speak elatedly about yourselves." Rather, according to the terms of the Law covenant, the qualified male members of only one family in Israel were made the priests, to serve in behalf of all the rest of the nation. This was the family of Moses' older brother, Aaron, of the tribe of Levi. He was made God's high priest, and his sons were made the underpriests. So they made up an Aaronic priesthood.

³⁰ The fit male members of all the rest of the families of the tribe of Levi were made ministers to the Aaronic priesthood, to aid them in carrying on the religious services at the house of God, or tent of meeting, that was provided for in the Law covenant. —Exodus 27:20 through 28:4; Numbers 3:1-13.

³¹ Thus the tribe of Judah had no share in the priesthood of ancient Israel, because from this tribe was to come the Messianic "leader," the one called "Shiloh"

---

to whom "the obedience of the peoples will belong." (Genesis 49:10; 1 Chronicles 5:2) So, in ancient Israel, the kingship and the priesthood were kept separate. Aaron and his sons were not made king-priests, thus being unlike Melchizedek.

[32] According to the Law covenant, three national festivals were to be celebrated by all the people at the tent or tabernacle of worship each year. "Three times in the year every male of yours should appear before Jehovah your God in the place that he will choose: in the festival of the unfermented cakes and the festival of weeks and the festival of booths, and none should appear before Jehovah empty-handed. The gift of each one's hand should be in proportion to the blessing of Jehovah your God that he has given you." (Deuteronomy 16:16, 17; Exodus 34:1, 22-24) The festival of the unleavened cakes was held in connection with the annual Passover supper that commemorated Israel's deliverance from Egypt. The festival of weeks was held on the fiftieth day, that is, after the passing of seven weeks beginning Nisan 16; and the firstfruits of the wheat harvest were presented to Jehovah on that fiftieth (or, Pentecostal) day. The festival of booths (or, tabernacles) was also called the "festival of the ingathering" at the turn of the year. These annual festivals had their prescribed sacrifices to Jehovah. —Leviticus 23:4-21, 33-43.

[33] Five days before the celebration of the festival of booths began, the annual "day of atonement" (*Yom Kippur*) was to be held, on the tenth day of the seventh lunar month as counted from the spring month of Nisan or Abib. That would be on Tishri 10. On this day an atonement would be made for the sins of the whole nation in covenant relationship with Jehovah, this being the one day of the year when the Aaronic high priest would go into the Most Holy of the tent of meeting and sprinkle the blood of the atonement victims (a bull and a goat) before the sacred ark of the covenant, which contained the written Law of Jehovah. (Leviticus 23:26-32; 16:2-34) Of course, the death and sprinkled blood of these subhuman animal victims could not real-

---

32. What festivals were to be celebrated annually by Israel?
33. When was the Day of Atonement held, and why did its sacrifices have to be repeated year after year?

ly take away the sins of humans to whom such animals were put in subjection. It was for the very reason that the death and blood of those sacrificed animals did not actually take away the sins of the human kind that the Atonement Day sacrifices had to be repeated year after year.

34 We can see the reason for this. In the Law covenant God plainly commanded: "If a fatal accident should occur, then you must give soul for soul, eye for eye, tooth for tooth, hand for hand, foot for foot, branding for branding, wound for wound, blow for blow." (Exodus 21:23-25; Deuteronomy 19:21) In other words, like should go for like, something of equal value for something of equal value. So an uncondemned human life would have to go for a human life that had come under condemnation. This is why it is written in Psalm 49:6-10: "Those who are trusting in their means of maintenance, and who keep boasting about the abundance of their riches, not one of them can by any means redeem even a brother, nor give to God a ransom for him; (and the redemption price of their soul is so precious that it has ceased to time indefinite) that he should still live forever and not see the pit. For he sees that even the wise ones die." There must be a corresponding ransom, and none of the sin-laden Israelites could provide that in order to redeem the perfect life that was forfeited by Adam.

35 The Aaronic priesthood that offered mere animal sacrifices at the sacred house of God passed away nineteen centuries ago, in the year 70 C.E. when Jerusalem and its temple were destroyed by the Roman armies. There is nothing else to do but look to the Messianic King whom Jehovah God swore to make a "priest to time indefinite according to the manner of Melchizedek!" (Psalm 110:1-4) This one should be the "seed" of God's heavenly "woman," the seed whom God appoints and enables to bruise the head of the wicked one symbolized by that "serpent" in Eden. If this one were not to provide the redemptive ransom for all mankind, then there is no help for us humans,

34. What did the Law covenant show that God required for taking away human sin, and why could no Israelite offer what was required?
35. What has happened to the Aaronic priesthood, and so where should the redemptive ransom sacrifice be looked for?

no outlook for eternal life in a righteous new order under Jehovah God. So, then, the animal sacrifices that were offered on Israel's "day of atonement" down to the first century C.E. must be pictorial; they must picture prophetically the needed ransom sacrifice that was to be offered by the Messiah who becomes the Melchizedekian priest, the Bruiser of the serpent's head.

36 Likewise with those annual festivals that God's covenant imposed upon ancient Israel. They were not mere meaningless occasions for national entertainment and relaxation. They had prophetic significance. Being happy occasions, they pictured the future happy provisions that God has made for mankind. The blessed meaning of them God makes known in his due time according to his "eternal purpose."

A NATION WITH WONDERFUL OPPORTUNITIES

37 However, could any Israelite gain eternal life for himself by keeping the Law of the covenant with God perfectly, without breaking even the slightest part of it? The Law covenant offered each Israelite the opportunity to prove that he could do so. In Leviticus 18:5 this opportunity is referred to, in these words: "You must keep my statutes and my judicial decisions, which if a man will do, he must also live by means of them. I am Jehovah." So, if any Israelite kept the Law flawlessly and gained eternal life by his own works, he did not need the benefit of the sacrifices of the Law covenant. Neither would he need the blessing of the Abrahamic Promise. (Genesis 12:3; 22:18) Such a perfect Law keeper would establish his own righteousness and life merit.

38 However, even the prophet Moses died. Even the high priest Aaron died. And every other Israelite from the establishment of the Law covenant down to the passing away of the Aaronic priesthood in the year 70 C.E., yes, down till today, has died. Even nineteen centuries since the destruction of Jerusalem's temple by the Romans the orthodox Israelites of today go

---

36. Likewise, how must the festivals held under the Law covenant be viewed?
37. What opportunity did the Law covenant offer to Israelites?
38, 39. (a) What shows whether any of the Israelites gained life by keeping the Law perfectly? (b) Whose priestly services before God are therefore needed?

through a form of celebrating the Day of Atonement or *Yom Kippur*. This in itself is an admission of their need of cleansing from sin, yes, their inability to keep the Law perfectly and gain eternal life by their own righteous works. And if *they* could not do this under the Law covenant, how could any of the rest of us imperfect humans do so?

[39] In view of what the Law covenant made plainly manifest, we all stand condemned before the God whose activity is perfect. (Deuteronomy 32:4) As the prophet Isaiah said more than seven hundred years after the Law covenant was made with Israel: "All our righteousnesses are as a polluted garment." (Isaiah 64:5, *JPS*) We all need the services of the promised Melchizedekian Priest, who is to be a priest forever.

[40] Turn back now to the year of the establishment of that covenant between Jehovah God and Israel by means of the mediator Moses. That lunar year ended, and Nisan 1 of the calendar year 1512 B.C.E. arrived. On that day Moses obeyed God's command and had the "tabernacle of the tent of meeting" set up for God's worship thereat to begin. Then Moses clothed his older brother Aaron and Aaron's sons with their official garments and anointed them with the holy anointing oil to serve as high priest and underpriests. "So Moses finished the work. And the cloud began to cover the tent of meeting, and Jehovah's glory filled the tabernacle. And Moses was not able to go into the tent of meeting, because the cloud resided over it and Jehovah's glory filled the tabernacle."—Exodus 40:1-35.

[41] There was the visible evidence that Jehovah had accepted this structure of worship and had sanctified it to His purpose. On the seventh day of that first month of Nisan (or, Abib) the installing and empowering of the Aaronic priesthood was completed, and thereafter they could officially supervise all features of divine worship at the sacred tabernacle.—Leviticus 8:1 through 9:24.

[42] Jehovah was the God whom that nation of Israel

---

40. What did Moses do on Nisan 1, 1512 B.C.E., with regard to God's worship, and what then happened?
41. Of what was that manifestation an evidence, and when was the installation of the priesthood completed?
42. Besides being their God for worship, what else was Jehovah then to Israel, without need of a visible representative?

was commanded and under obligation to worship. He
was not alone their God. He was also their royal
Ruler, their King, to whom they owed submission and
loyalty. Disobedience to His laws and commandments
would therefore be insubordination and disloyalty. Con-
firming that fact, in Deuteronomy 33:5 the prophet
Moses refers to the nation of Israel as Jeshurun or
"Upright One" because of its entering into the Law
covenant and says: "And there was a king in Jeshurun,
when the heads of the people were gathered, all the
tribes of Israel together." (Translation by The Jewish
Publication Society of America) And, says the editorial
footnote on that verse by the late Dr. J. H. Hertz,
C. H.: "Thus began God's Kingdom over Israel." (*Pentateuch and Haftorahs*, Soncino Press, page 910) Jehovah was their invisible heavenly King. He needed
no earthly visible human king to represent Him in
Israel.—Genesis 36:31.

43 How highly favored was this nation that was made
up of the descendants of Abraham, Isaac and Jacob
(Israel) and that had been brought into a covenant
with the one living and true God! They had his true
worship and enjoyed the prospect of becoming to Him
a "kingdom of priests and a holy nation."

44 Said the prophet Amos: "Hear this word that
Jehovah has spoken concerning you, O sons of Israel,
concerning the whole family that I brought up out of
the land of Egypt, saying, 'You people only have I
known out of all the families of the ground.'" (Amos
3:1, 2) It was an accurate comparison that the psalmist
expressed in one of the Hallelujah psalms, saying: "He
is telling his word to Jacob, his regulations and his
judicial decisions to Israel. He has not done that way to
any other nation; and as for his judicial decisions, they
have not known them. Praise Jah, you people!" (Psalm
147:19, 20) The favored nation indeed had good reason
to praise Jehovah by keeping his covenant. Whether
they did so was now to be shown during what might
be called the Era of the Law Covenant that had now
begun.

43, 44. How uniquely had ancient Israel been favored in comparison with all other earthly nations, and how could they therefore
praise Jehovah?

CHAPTER 10

A Covenant for a Kingdom Made with David

GOD marks off his own time periods according to His "eternal purpose." One such time period is marked off for us in the book of 1 Kings, chapter six, verse one, where it is written: "And it came about in the four hundred and eightieth year after the sons of Israel came out from the land of Egypt, in the fourth year, in the month of Ziv, the second month, after Solomon became king over Israel, that he proceeded to build the house to Jehovah." This was an appropriate measurement of time, for it was from when the Israelites were delivered from Egypt, shortly after which they began to build the house of worship in the wilderness of Sinai, to when King Solomon the son of David began to build the temple at Jerusalem. This was from Nisan 15, 1513 B.C.E., to 1034 B.C.E., Ziv (or, Iyyar) 1.—Numbers 33:1-4; 1 Kings 6:37.

2 Of course, much had happened during those almost five centuries. Because of a lack of faith in God's ability to subdue the nations that then inhabited the Promised Land, the Israelites were obliged to wander in the wilderness of Sinai for almost forty years. During that time the older Israelites who had revolted against invading the Promised Land under God's leadership in the second year of their exodus died off. (Numbers 13:1 through 14:38) At the end of forty years God miraculously brought them across the flooding Jordan River into the Promised Land, the land of Canaan.

3 Then, under the leadership of Joshua, the successor of Moses, there began years of warfare for subduing the land. According to the words of faithful Caleb, the

---

1. What time period is marked off in 1 Kings 6:1, and why is this time measurement appropriate?
2, 3. (a) Why did the Israelites wander so long in the wilderness of Sinai? (b) How long were they in subduing the Promised Land, after which how were they ruled for centuries?

son of Jephunneh of the tribe of Judah, at the time of apportioning out the occupied land to the families of Israel, the Israelites were six years in subduing the land and dispossessing its inhabitants. (Joshua 14:1-10) After that God gave the now settled Israelites a line of judges for centuries until a change in the form of the national government was introduced in the days of the prophet Samuel. A Jewish chronologer of nineteen hundred years ago briefly measured out this period for us. Speaking one sabbath day in a synagogue in Antioch of Pisidia, Asia Minor, this chronologer said:

⁴ "Men of Israel, and ye that fear God, hearken. The God of this people Israel chose our fathers, and exalted the people when they sojourned in the land of Egypt, and with a high arm led he them forth out of it. And for about the time of forty years suffered he their manners in the wilderness. And when he had destroyed seven nations in the land of Canaan, he gave them their land for an inheritance, for about four hundred and fifty years [all that during about four hundred and fifty years, *NW*]: and after these things he gave them judges until Samuel the prophet. And afterward they asked for a king; and God gave unto them Saul the son of Kish, a man of the tribe of Benjamin, for the space of forty years."—Acts 13:14-21, English Revised Version Bible, published in England in 1884 C.E. See also the Douay Version Bible, published in 1610 C.E. Also, *The Emphasised Bible*, by J. B. Rotherham, published in 1897 C.E.

⁵ The allotting of the land to Caleb and the other Israelites for an inheritance took place in the year 1467 B.C.E. If we measure back "about four hundred and fifty years" it brings us to the year 1918 B.C.E. This was the year in which Isaac, the son of Abraham by Sarah, was born and God chose Isaac instead of Ishmael, the older son of Abraham by Sarah's Egyptian maidservant Hagar. With a sworn oath God had confirmed to Isaac the covenant He had made with Abraham for the possession of the land of Canaan, and now here at the end of this four-hundred-and-fifty-year

---

4, 5. (a) What time period did that Bible chronologer mark off in Israel's history before they had judges? (b) With what events did that time period begin and end?

period God was allotting to Isaac's offspring for an inheritance that Promised Land. In faithfulness Jehovah God was adhering to his "eternal purpose" for blessing all mankind.

6 During the period of the fifteen judges from Joshua to Samuel, the men of Israel tried to persuade the sixth judge, Gideon, the son of Joash of the tribe of Manasseh, to set up a dynasty of rulers in his family, instead of having Jehovah God as King. But Gideon was loyal to the Sovereign Ruler of Israel and turned down the offer of rulership, saying: "I myself shall not rule over you, nor will my son rule over you. Jehovah is the one who will rule over you." (Judges 8:22, 23) One of Gideon's many sons, named Abimelech (meaning "My Father Is King"), influenced the landowners of Shechem to install him as king over them. He came under God's adverse judgments and, after he had reigned for three years, a woman brought about his death in battle.—Judges 9:1-57.

A KING OVER ALL ISRAEL

7 In the old age of the fifteenth judge, Samuel the prophet, the elders of Israel came to him with the request: "Now do appoint for us a king to judge us like all the nations." Samuel took this as a rejection of him as God's appointed judge, but Jehovah said to him: "Listen to the voice of the people as respects all that they say to you; for it is not you whom they have rejected, but it is I whom they have rejected from being king over them." God told Samuel to warn the Israelites of all the hardship that it would mean for them to have a visible human king, but they still expressed preference for such a king. God, as the Sovereign Lord over Israel, did the choosing of the man to be Israel's first human king. He sent Samuel to anoint Saul the son of Kish of the tribe of Benjamin to be the king. In the year 1117 B.C.E. Saul was installed as king at the city of Mizpah. "The people began to shout and say: 'Let the king live!'" Saul

---

6. (a) How did Judge Gideon show loyalty to God's sovereignty? (b) How did Gideon's son Abimelech fare as a king?
7. When and how did Israel come to have a human king chosen by God, and how long did he reign?

reigned for forty years.—1 Samuel 8:1 through 10:25; Acts 13:21.*

8 In the eleventh year of Saul's reign there occurred a seemingly insignificant event in the city of Bethlehem in the territory of the tribe of Judah. Jesse the Bethlehemite became father to an eighth son, whom he named David. Little did King Saul or anyone else in Israel know that this newborn baby would one day become so illustrious that his birthplace, Bethlehem, would one day be called "the city of David." No one then knew that, some three hundred years later, it would be prophesied concerning that city of David: "But thou, Beth-lechem Ephratah, the least though thou be among the thousands of Judah, yet out of thee shall he come forth unto me that is to be ruler in Israel, whose origin is from olden times, from most ancient days." (Micah 5:1, *Leeser; JPS;* 5:2, *NEB; NW*) This prophecy the Jewish religious leaders of the first century before our Common Era understood to apply to the Messiah. So the "seed" of God's "woman" was to be born in Bethlehem.

9 However, prior to this, after King Saul had reigned for two years, he yielded to a lack of faith and acted presumptuously, indiscreetly, in office. "At this Samuel said to Saul: 'You have acted foolishly. You have not kept the commandment of Jehovah your God that he commanded you, because, if you had, Jehovah would have made your kingdom firm over Israel to time indefinite. And now your kingdom will not last. Jehovah will certainly find for himself a man agreeable to his heart; and Jehovah will commission him as a leader over his people, because you did not keep what Jehovah commanded you.' " (1 Samuel 13:1-14) The "man agreeable to [God's] heart" was not yet born, for those words were spoken years before the birth of David at

---

* In *Antiquities of the Jews*, Book 10, chapter 8, paragraph 4, Flavius Josephus of the first century C.E. assigns twenty years to King Saul. But in Book 6, chapter 14, paragraph 9, Josephus wrote: "Now Saul, reigned eighteen years while Samuel was alive, and after his death two," to which some Josephus manuscripts add: "and twenty"; making a total of forty years.

8. (a) In the eleventh year of Saul's reign, what birth occurred in Bethlehem? (b) What did Micah prophesy about Bethlehem?
9. In view of Saul's indiscretion, what did God have Samuel tell Saul about the kingdom, and whom would God choose for the throne?

Bethlehem. This made it evident that the Most High God would exercise his power and right and make his own choice of an Israelite to succeed King Saul. In doing so he would stick to his "eternal purpose" in connection with the Messiah.

[10] When David was just a teen-age shepherd boy at Bethlehem, God designated him as the man agreeable to his heart. Although David was not Jesse's firstborn but was merely the eighth son, God sent Samuel to Bethlehem to anoint David to become the future king of Israel.

[11] David came into the spotlight when he alone of all the Israelites volunteered to meet the challenging Philistine giant Goliath on the field of battle and killed him with a slingstone aimed at Goliath's forehead. (1 Samuel 16:1 through 17:58) David was taken into King Saul's army, and his popularity with the people grew beyond that of the king. This made Saul very jealous and he tried to kill David and thus prevent him from supplanting one of his own sons on the throne of Israel. Eventually a fatal wound in battle, followed by his falling upon his own sword to speed his death, ended Saul's kingship. Ish-bosheth, the surviving son of Saul, was made king by those cleaving to Saul's family line, but only over eleven tribes of Israel. The tribesmen of Judah anointed David king over them in Hebron in the territory of Judah. That was in the year 1077 B.C.E.—2 Samuel 2:1-11; Acts 13:21, 22.

[12] Saul's son Ish-bosheth lasted on the throne of Israel possibly for seven years and six months and then he was assassinated by subjects of his. (2 Samuel 2:11 through 4:8) All the tribes now recognized David as Jehovah's chosen one and they anointed David as king over all Israel, at Hebron. This was in the year 1070 B.C.E. (2 Samuel 4:9 through 5:5) Thus, in harmony with Jacob's deathbed prophecy as recorded in Genesis 49:10, the "scepter" and the "commander's staff" had come to the tribe of Judah. On what basis,

---

10, 11. (a) How was David designated to be the future king of Israel? (b) How did David incur Saul's murderous jealousy, and where did he first become a king?
12. When and how was David made king over all Israel, and what question arises now as to the "scepter" and "commander's staff"?

now, would those emblems of royalty not "turn aside from Judah . . . until Shiloh comes"?

[13] Because of three anointings for kingship, King David could really be called an "anointed one" or "messiah" (Hebrew: *ma·shi'ahh*), as in 2 Samuel 19:21, 22; 22:51; 23:1. Outstandingly, David was used as a prophetic type of the preeminent Messiah, the "seed" of God's heavenly "woman." (See Ezekiel 34:23.) In fact, God saw good to choose David to be in the line of descent that culminated in the Messiah of God's "eternal purpose." How did this occur?

[14] Shortly after being anointed king over reunited Israel in 1070 B.C.E., David captured the city of Jebus from the Jebusites and called it Jerusalem. There he moved his government and made this lofty city his capital, it being more centrally located than Hebron, for it was at the borderline between the territories of Judah and Benjamin. (Judges 1:21; 2 Samuel 5:6-10; 1 Chronicles 11:4-9) Not long after that, King David gave consideration to the sacred Ark of Jehovah. For decades it had been allowed to be displaced from the Most Holy of the tent of meeting at Shiloh in the territory of Ephraim. (1 Samuel 1:24; 4:3-18; 6:1 through 7:2) David felt that the Ark should be in the capital city. So he had it brought up and lodged in a tent near his palace.—2 Samuel 6:1-19.

[15] However, David came to feel embarrassed, because he, a mere human king, dwelt in a royal palace whereas the Ark of Jehovah, the true God and real King of Israel, dwelt in a modest tent. To put matters in proper balance, David conceived the idea of building a worthy house, a temple, to the Most High God and Universal Sovereign. But Jehovah disapproved of David's building such a temple. By His prophet Nathan he told David that a peaceful son of his would be privileged to build the temple at Jerusalem. Then, in appreciation for David's heartfelt devotion to God's pure worship, Jehovah did a wonderful thing with this man who was "agreeable to his heart." Of His

---

13. How was David really an "anointed one," and of whom was he made a prophetic type?
14. What city did David make the capital of all Israel, and what sacred object did he then locate there?
15. What covenant did Jehovah now establish toward David, and out of appreciation for what on David's part?

own accord, he established a covenant toward David for an everlasting kingdom. He said:

"Jehovah has told you that a house is what Jehovah will make for you. When your days come to the full, and you must lie down with your forefathers, then I shall certainly raise up your seed after you, which will come out of your inward parts; and I shall indeed firmly establish his kingdom. He is the one that will build a house for my name, and I shall certainly establish the throne of his kingdom firmly to time indefinite. I myself shall become his father, and he himself will become my son. When he does wrong, I will also reprove him with the rod of men and with the strokes of the sons of Adam. As for my loving-kindness, it will not depart from him the way I removed it from Saul, whom I removed on account of you. And your house and your kingdom will certainly be steadfast to time indefinite before you; your very throne will become one firmly established to time indefinite."—2 Samuel 7:1-16; 1 Chronicles 17:1-15.

16 David offered a prayer of gratitude and closed it, saying:

"And now, O Sovereign Lord Jehovah, you are the true God; and as for your words, let them prove to be truth, since you promise to your servant this goodness. And now take it upon yourself and bless the house of your servant for it to continue to time indefinite before you; for you yourself, O Sovereign Lord Jehovah, have promised, and due to your blessing let the house of your servant be blessed to time indefinite." —2 Samuel 7:18-29; 1 Chronicles 17:16-27.

17 That covenant promise to David was backed by God's oath:

"Jehovah has sworn to David, truly he will not draw back from it: 'Of the fruitage of your belly I shall set on your throne. If your sons will keep my covenant and my reminders that I shall teach them, their sons also forever will sit upon your throne.'"—Psalm 132:11, 12.

"To time indefinite I shall preserve my loving-kindness toward him, and my covenant will be faithful to him. And I shall certainly set up his seed forever and his throne as the days of heaven. . . . I shall not profane my covenant, and the expression out of my lips I shall not change. Once I have sworn in my holiness, to David I will not tell lies. His seed itself will prove to be even to time indefinite, and his throne as the sun in front of me."—Psalm 89:28-36. See also Jeremiah 33:20, 21.

18 According to that covenant toward King David, his kingdom had to furnish the basis for the coming kingdom of the Greater Messiah. That is why the

---

16. What prayer of gratitude did David offer to Jehovah for this?
17. This covenant was also backed up by what on God's part?
18. The prophecy of Isaiah declares that David's kingdom would furnish the basis for what greater kingdom?

prophet Isaiah, centuries later, was inspired to prophesy: "For a child is born to us, a son given to us, and the rulership is upon his shoulder; and his name is called: Wonder, Counselor, Strong God, Everlasting Father, Prince of Peace; in order that the rulership may increase and there may be no end of peace upon the throne of David and in his kingdom; to rear it up and to support it through what is suitable and what is right from now on to forever. The zeal of the Eternal One of armies does such a thing."—Isaiah 9:5, 6, according to the translation of the Hebrew scholar Rabbi Leopold Pheinkard Zunz, German, sixteenth edition of 1913 C.E. See Isaiah 9:6, 7, *AV; RS; NEB; Jerusalem Bible.*

[19] According to the prophecy of Micah 5:1 (*Zunz; 5:2, AV; NW*), this Messianic child was to be born, this royal son was to be given, at Bethlehem in Ephrathah in the territory of Judah. This place of human birth was to be one of the identifying marks of the true Messiah, the "seed" of God's figurative "woman." Bethlehem, and not the royal city of Jerusalem, was the birthplace of his ancestor, King David, and hence came to be called David's city.

A DYNASTY OF DAVIDIC KINGS

[20] In fulfillment of this kingdom covenant toward David, there followed a line of kings of Jerusalem all in the family line of King David. Counted from David's kingship in Jerusalem in 1070 B.C.E. this kingdom with a dynasty of Davidic kings in Jerusalem lasted for 463 years, or till 607 B.C.E. So this means that, when we count from the year 1117 B.C.E., when the prophet Samuel anointed Saul as king over all Israel, the nation of Israel had visible kings for 510 years. However, Jehovah was the invisible King.

[21] As the royal representative of God who had chosen and anointed him to be king over Israel, King David sat on "Jehovah's throne" at Jerusalem. (1 Chronicles

19. According to Micah's prophecy, this "child" was to be born in what city, and this as an identification mark of whom?
20. How long did David's dynasty last on the throne, and how long did the Israelites have kings?
21. Did David ascend to heaven at death, and who did David prophesy would be invited to sit down at God's right hand?

29:23) But he did not sit at Jehovah's right hand, for Jehovah's throne is in the heavens. (Isaiah 66:1) At his death in 1037 B.C.E., David did not ascend into the spirit heavens and sit down at Jehovah's right hand up there. He was not invited to do so; but down to the first century of our Common Era the Israelites could locate and identify David's burial place. Rather, David himself was inspired by God to prophesy, in Psalm 110:1-4, that his Messianic descendant who would be like King-Priest Melchizedek would be the one whom Jehovah would invite to sit down at His right hand in the heavens.

²² David's young son, Solomon, followed him upon the throne of Jerusalem, "Jehovah's throne." According to the divine promise, he was the one favored with building the temple on Mount Moriah at Jerusalem, completing it in the year 1027 B.C.E. (1 Kings 6:1-38) In Solomon's old age he became unfaithful to the God whose temple he had constructed. The majority of his successors on the throne of Jerusalem also turned out bad. The last of these Davidic kings to sit on Jerusalem's throne was Zedekiah. For his rebellion against the king of Babylon, who had made Zedekiah a tributary king, he was carried off captive to Babylon, but leaving the city of Jerusalem and its gorgeous temple behind in ruins. (2 Kings 24:17 through 25:21) Never since that tragic year of 607 B.C.E. has there been a Davidic king upon Jerusalem's throne.

²³ Did that signify that the kingdom covenant toward David had failed or had been canceled? By no means! God gave assurance against that. About the fourth year before the dethronement of Zedekiah and his being exiled in Babylon, God inspired his prophet Ezekiel to say to this last king on Jerusalem's throne:

"As for you, O deadly wounded, wicked chieftain of Israel, whose day has come in the time of the error of the end, this is what the Sovereign Lord Jehovah has said, 'Remove the turban, and lift off the crown. This will not be the same. Put on high even what is low, and bring low even the high one. A ruin, a ruin, a ruin I shall make it. As for this also,

22. How did Solomon and the majority of his successors on the throne turn out, and since when has Jerusalem not had a Davidic king on the throne?
23. Had the kingdom covenant failed or been canceled, and what assurance did God give by Ezekiel about this?

it will certainly become no·one's until he comes who has the legal right, and I must give it to him.' "—Ezekiel 21:25-27.

²⁴ Do we get the drift of that? Jehovah himself would make a ruin of the kingdom of the royal family of David at Jerusalem. Things would not be the same as formerly. The Gentile ruling powers that had been low in God's sight would be put on top, and the earthly kingdom of Jehovah's chosen people would be brought low, in subjection to the Gentile world powers. The period of Gentile world supremacy without interference from a typical kingdom of God at Jerusalem would continue on until the coming of the one "who has the legal right," that is to say, the promised true Messiah, and the Sovereign Lord Jehovah would give the kingdom to him. The Gentile world powers would then be no longer on top to dominate the earth. The Messianic kingdom would take world control. Thus, according to the covenant established toward David, his kingdom would be an everlasting government. His throne must stand forever!

²⁵ So, even though down to this very day no Davidic throne has been reestablished at Jerusalem in the Middle East, all is not lost for those hoping in the promised Messiah, the "seed" of God's heavenly "woman." True, by the autumn of 607 B.C.E. the throne city of Jerusalem and its temple lay in ruins. The nearby city of Bethlehem, David's city, lay in ruins at the hands of the Babylonian conquerors. Still, the Law covenant made with Israel at Mount Sinai in Arabia continued in operation. Also, the covenant for an everlasting kingdom as established toward David continued to apply. God's "eternal purpose" in connection with his Messiah stood. God's kingdom covenant will not fail. Neither his purpose!

---

24. What was to be brought low, and when was the reverse of this to take place, and how?
25. Despite Jerusalem's desolation in 607 B.C.E., what covenants and purpose still stood?

CHAPTER 11

The Messiah
of God's "Eternal Purpose"

RESURRECTION of a city that had lain dead in ruins for seventy years—in the year 537 B.C.E.! The city was Jerusalem that had been destroyed by the Babylonians in 607 B.C.E. When this holy city rose from the dust, there was a rebirth of the land of Judah, yes, the rebirth of a nation, the repatriated people of Jehovah God. (Isaiah 66:8) It was marvelous in the eyes of all observers.

² Along with this national resurrection the hopes for the coming of the promised Messiah were revived. (Ezekiel 37:1-14) Even during the seventy years that the people of the kingdom of Judah were in exile in the land of Babylon the fixed time for the arrival of the Messiah was indicated to them. This Messiah was to be someone later than the Persian conqueror, Cyrus the Great, concerning whom the prophet Isaiah had been inspired to say: "This is what Jehovah has said to his anointed one [Hebrew: ma·shi'ahh], to Cyrus, whose right hand I have taken hold of, to subdue before him nations, so that I may ungird even the hips of kings; to open before him the two-leaved doors, so that even the gates will not be shut." (Isaiah 45:1) As Jehovah's anointed agent, Cyrus had come and got through the gates of the highly walled city of Babylon and had overthrown and killed its imperial ruler Belshazzar, the son of Nabonidus. That was in 539 B.C.E. But Cyrus did not at once release the exiled Israelites. He took over the kingship of Babylon and held the Jews captive about two years more, till 537 B.C.E. Thus seventy years were fulfilled!

³ This was just as had been foretold in Jeremiah 25:11. And 2 Chronicles 36:20, 21 made a historical

---

1. When did a rebirth of a land and of a nation occur?
2. (a) The coming promised Messiah was to be later than what anointed agent of Jehovah? (b) How were seventy years of exile fulfilled though Babylon fell in 539 B.C.E.?
3. How long did the desolate land of Judah keep sabbath?

130

record of this, saying: "Furthermore, he carried off those remaining from the sword captive to Babylon, and they came to be servants to him and his sons until the royalty of Persia began to reign; to fulfill Jehovah's word by the mouth of Jeremiah, until the land [of Judah] had paid off its sabbaths. All the days of lying desolated it kept sabbath, to fulfill seventy years"—from 607 B.C.E. to 537 B.C.E.

4 Among the exiled Jews in Babylon was Daniel the prophet. From the inspired writings of Jeremiah, Daniel did not expect the release from exile to come for the Jews until at the end of the seventy years that Jerusalem lay desolate in sabbath keeping. (Daniel 9:1, 2) So during the first year of the new Medo-Persian regime over the Babylonian Empire, Daniel prayed about the matter. It was then that Jehovah's angel Gabriel arrived and gave Daniel the following information regarding the time for Messiah to come:

"Seventy (year-) weeks have been appointed over you people and over your holy city, to restrain the apostasy and to make an end of sin, and to atone for the error, and to bring everlasting salvation, that vision and prophecy may be sealed, and the Most Holy be anointed.

"And you may know and understand: From the going forth of the decree to rebuild Jerusalem until the Anointed One, the Prince, there are seven (year-) weeks; also sixty-two (year-) weeks, so market place and moat will be rebuilt, and that in the pressure of the times.

"And after the sixty-two (year-) weeks an Anointed One will be destroyed, and he has no (successor), and a people of the coming prince will destroy the city and the sanctuary, and his end is coming as by ripping, and war and desolation are ordained till the end.

"And he will conclude a strong covenant with many, for one (year-) week, and at the half of the (year-) week he will cancel sacrifice and oblation, and beside the wing (places) a frightful abomination, and that is until the desolation, the one firmly determined upon, is poured out upon the desolator."
—Daniel 9:24-27, Zunz; see also Moffatt.

"MORNING" OF SEVENTH CREATIVE "DAY"
BEGINS, 526 B.C.E.

5 The first half or "evening" period of God's seventh creative "day" was now closing, 3,500 years from

4. (a) When did Daniel calculate that the end of the Jewish exile would come? (b) What information did Gabriel give Daniel about the time of Messiah's coming?
5. How is the calculation made of when the seven plus the sixty-two "weeks of years" ended?

creation of Adam and Eve. The morning of this creative "day" was due to begin at 526 B.C.E. From then on things should brighten with regard to God's purpose and for His people. According to Daniel's prophecy, from a certain feature in the rebuilding of the resurrected city of Jerusalem seventy "(year-) weeks" or "weeks of years" (amounting to 490 years) would count. "Seven (year-) weeks" plus "sixty-two (year-) weeks" would run for a total of 483 years until the coming of the Anointed One (Hebrew: *Ma·shi'ahh*). Counted from when the Jewish governor Nehemiah rebuilt the walls of Jerusalem, these sixty-nine "weeks of years" would end in the first half of the first century of our Common Era. Counted from the twentieth year of King Artaxerxes (455 B.C.E.), the year in which Nehemiah rebuilt those walls, the 483 years would end in the year 29 of our Common Era. (Nehemiah 2:1-18) That was about forty-one years before the second destruction of Jerusalem, this time by the Romans. Did something historic happen in 29 C.E.?

⁶ Both the first century C.E. and the first century B.C.E. were critical years for the Israelites in Palestine. In the fourth century B.C.E. the control of the repatriated Israelites or Jews had passed out of the hands of the Persian emperor into the hands of the Grecian Empire, due to the conquests of the Macedonian Alexander the Great. In the year 332 B.C.E. he gained control of Palestine and left Jerusalem untouched. Then he overthrew the Persian emperor and established the Grecian World Power, the fifth one of Bible history. In that same year Alexander gave orders for the city of Alexandria to be built in conquered Egypt. This became a flourishing city and a large Jewish population grew up there. These came to speak the common Greek language, which had now become a language internationally known and used as a result of Alexander's conquests. They also desired Bible knowledge.

⁷ So, during the following century, about 280 B.C.E., they began the work of having their sacred inspired

6. How was the Persian Empire overthrown, and how did Alexandria, Egypt, come to play a part in Jewish life?
7. How did the Greek *Septuagint Version* come to be produced, and how does it read at Daniel 9:25, 26?

Scriptures, from Genesis to Malachi, translated into their own common Greek language. It was completed by the first century B.C.E. and came to be called "The Greek Septuagint Version." In view of the wide usage of the common Greek even during the first centuries of the Roman Empire, this translation by those Alexandrian Jews could be used internationally. It reflected the Hebrew Bible text quite faithfully. For example, the Greek rendering of Daniel 9:25, 26 read (according to Bagster's English translation) concerning the Messiah (*Ma·shi'ahh*):

> "And thou shalt know and understand, that from the going forth of the command for the answer and for the building of Jerusalem until Christ the prince there shall be seven weeks, and sixty-two weeks: and then the time shall return, and the street shall be built, and the wall, and the times shall be exhausted. And after the sixty-two weeks, the anointed one shall be destroyed, and there is no judgment in him: . . ."

[8] The common Greek continued to be the ancient world's international language even after the Grecian World Power fell before the Roman World Power in the first century B.C.E. One wing of the Maccabean contenders for power in Jerusalem appealed for aid from Rome against the other wing, and so in the year 63 B.C.E. the Roman general Pompey invaded and took control of Jerusalem, and Palestine came under Roman control. In 40 B.C.E. the Jews regained kingship. However, in 37 B.C.E. Herod the Great, a descendant of Esau or Edom, attacked Jerusalem and captured it and ruled as king, as Rome's appointee. In the first century C.E., the Jews rebelled again against Rome, in 66 C.E., but their short-lived independence was brought to an end in 70 C.E. by the destruction of Jerusalem and its glorious temple rebuilt by Herod the Great. Since then, or for more than nineteen centuries now, the Jews have had no temple at Jerusalem, even since the Republic of Israel was established in 1948 C.E. Besides that, the Israelis acknowledge no prophet as from God since Malachi of the fifth century B.C.E., or more than 2,400 years ago. Is that not strange? What is wrong?

---

8. (a) How did Jerusalem come under Roman control and later get destroyed? (b) For how long have the Jews had no temple at Jerusalem or not acknowledged a prophet as from God?

FULFILLMENT OF BIBLE PROPHECY
EXPLAINS MATTERS

⁹ When ancient Jerusalem was reestablished in 537 B.C.E., another city was restored in the land of Judah —Bethlehem. In Nehemiah 7:5-26, the governor of Jerusalem tells us of the remnant of Jews who returned to their homeland in 537 B.C.E., saying:

"Then I found the book of genealogical enrollment of those who came up at the first, and found written in it:

"These are the sons of the jurisdictional district who came up out of the captivity of the exiled people whom Nebuchadnezzar the king of Babylon had taken into exile and who later returned to Jerusalem and to Judah, each to his own city; those who came in with Zerubbabel, Jeshua [Greek *Septuagint*: Jesus], Nehemiah, . . . The number of the men of the people of Israel: . . . the men of Bethlehem and Netophah, a hundred and eighty-eight; . . ."—See also Ezra 2:21.

¹⁰ Thus there came into existence again the city of Bethlehem, "the city of David," in which it was possible for the Messianic prophecy of Micah 5:1 (*Leeser;* 5:2, Greek *Septuagint*) to be fulfilled. Since all independent human life from Cain and Abel onward begins at birth, Micah's prophecy makes us look for a certain birth in the rebuilt Bethlehem. This is to be a foretold birth. Now, when Isaac, the son of Abraham and Sarah, was to be born by a miracle, three angels of God visited them and announced the birth for the coming year, the leading angel saying: "Is anything too extraordinary for Jehovah?" (Genesis 18:1-14) Centuries afterward, when Samson, the physically strongest man ever on earth, was to be born to a till-then barren Israelitess, God's angel appeared first to the prospective mother and then to both her and her childless husband, to announce the coming birth of an outstanding judge in Israel. (Judges 13:1-20) Should anybody consider it strange, unbelievable, that what was to be the birth of all human births, the miraculous birth of the Messiah, would be announced to humans by heavenly angels?

¹¹ According to Jehovah's prophecy at Genesis 3:15, the "seed" that would bruise the Serpent's head fatally

---

9. When Jerusalem was reestablished in 537 B.C.E., what other city of importance was restored?
10. (a) Bethlehem thus became available for the fulfillment of what prophecy? (b) Why should it not be unbelievable that the promised birth there should be announced by angels?
11. According to Genesis 3:15, the one chosen for the earthly Messianic role would be taken from where?

was to be from God's heavenly "woman," that is, his wifelike organization of holy heavenly "sons of the true God." From that organization God could choose the particular spirit son for the earthly Messianic role.

12 What was the name of this favored son? An interesting question! But for the birth of this chosen son who was to be born into the human family at Bethlehem in the land of Judah, a human mother would be needed. Not only would she have to be of the tribe of Judah, but she would have to be a descendant of King David and thus be able to transmit a natural claim to David's kingdom. What girl whose native city was Bethlehem in Judah met the requirements? And what about a human husband for her, also of the royal family line of David? And was there an angelic announcement of the birth of one greater than Isaac? The historical record, as written by personal friends of the girl, answers these vital questions.

13 The time is now toward the end of the first century before our Common Era. Herod the Great, son of Antipater II, was still king in Jerusalem. Heli, a man of Davidic lineage, had moved from Bethlehem in the province of Judea up north to Nazareth in the province of Galilee. There a daughter of his, named Miriam (Hebrew) or Mariam (also Maria) in Greek, grew to marriageable age. She became engaged to marry a man of David's royal lineage, named Joseph, a carpenter in Nazareth but also a native of Bethlehem. This obliged her to remain virgin. But months before the wedding night, something remarkable occurred. To Maria or Mary there appeared an angel, who identified himself as Gabriel. After a greeting, he said:

14 "Have no fear, Mary, for you have found favor with God; and, look! you will conceive in your womb and give birth to a son, and you are to call his name Jesus [Hebrew: *Jeshua*]. This one will be great and will be called Son of the Most High; and Jehovah God will give him the throne of David his father, and he will rule as king over the house of Jacob forever, and there will be no end of his kingdom."—Luke 1: 26-33.

---

12. What questions now arise concerning the girl to be the human mother of the Messiah, and also concerning her husband?
13, 14. (a) Where was the suitable virgin Jewess found? (b) After greeting her, what did the angel Gabriel say?

¹⁵ According to the angel's statement, Mary's son was to be really the promised Messiah. He was to be called with the same name as that of the high priest who returned with Zerubbabel from Babylon in 537 B.C.E., namely, Jeshua, or, in Greek, Jesus. Because of birth through Mary he was to be called the son of "David his father." Accordingly, Jehovah God would give him the throne or royal seat of King David. As with David, his kingly rule would be over "the house of Jacob," that is, over all Israel. Since his kingly rule would be forever and there would be "no end of his kingdom," this meant that Jehovah God would fulfill in him the covenant that Jehovah had made toward David for an everlasting kingdom. He would thus need no successor. (2 Samuel 7:11-16) But how, and why, could he be called "Son of the Most High"? This one would not be the Most High God himself, who is Jehovah, but would be a Son of that Supreme One; and yet, how?

¹⁶ Mary herself inquired about this, saying: "How is this to be, since I am having no intercourse with a man?" Gabriel answered: "Holy spirit will come upon you, and power of the Most High will overshadow you. For that reason also what is born will be called holy, God's Son. And, look! Elizabeth your relative has also herself conceived a son, in her old age, and this is the sixth month for her, the so-called barren woman; because with God no declaration will be an impossibility."—Luke 1:34-37.

¹⁷ Did what was there declared to Mary prove to be an impossibility? This Jewish virgin was an example for us today in believing that it would not prove to be impossible for the Most High God. So she responded to the angel Gabriel: "Look! Jehovah's slave girl! May it take place with me according to your declaration." (Luke 1:38) Doubtless, at Mary's acceptance of God's will for her, conception took place within her, yet virgin. Holy spirit came upon her, and power of the Most High God overshadowed her. How was miraculous conception brought about thereby?

15. (a) What covenant made toward David was to be fulfilled in Mary's son? (b) His being "Son of the Most High" meant what?
16. In answer to Mary's inquiry as to how this could take place, what did Gabriel say?
17. When did the miraculous conception within Mary take place?

¹⁸ In this case an absolutely new living creature without any previous experience‧ or background was not brought into existence, as in the case of ordinary human conception by means of a human father. God's heavenly "woman," God's womanlike heavenly organization, had to be taken into account. Really from her the "seed" mentioned in Genesis 3:15 had to come. So she had to provide one of her spirit sons for this earthly assignment, for the "seed" to be bruised in the heel by the Serpent.

¹⁹ This did not mean that, for the Jewish virgin girl Mary to conceive, one of the heavenly spirit sons of God had to be sent to crawl into the microscopic ovum or egg cell in Mary's body and fertilize it. Such a thing is unreasonable, an absurdity! Rather, the Almighty God, the heavenly Father, by means of his holy spirit, transferred the life-force of his chosen heavenly son from the invisible spirit realm to the egg cell in Mary's body and fertilized it. In this way Mary became pregnant, and the child conceived in her was "holy." It was indeed what the angel Gabriel called it, the "Son of the Most High."—Luke 1:32.

²⁰ Who, though, was the son whom God chose to be born as a perfect human creature? It was not the angel Gabriel, for he was the one that materialized and appeared to Mary and announced her coming motherhood. The Holy Scriptures do indicate that it was the one whom an angel, when speaking to the prophet Daniel, called "the prince of you people," "the great prince who is standing in behalf of the sons of your people," namely, Michael. (Daniel 10:21; 12:1) He had been acting as a princely supervisory angel in behalf of the nation of Israel, and he was doubtless the angel that manifested himself in the burning thornbush to Moses at the foot of Mount Horeb back in the sixteenth century B.C.E. He has rightly been called Michael the archangel.* His having his life-force transferred to

---

* See Jude, verse 9; Revelation 12:7. For an earlier and fuller discussion of this, see the work by E. W. Hengstenberg, entitled "Christology of the Old Testament and Commentary," Volume 4, pages 301-304 (published in 1836-1839 C.E.).

18, 19. (a) Why, at Mary's conceiving, was it not the giving a start to an absolutely new creature without background? (b) Whose son could it rightly be called?
20. (a) Which son of God's heavenly organization was chosen? (b) How was he made available for the fulfillment of Isaiah 53:10?

Mary's egg cell by Almighty God's power that over-shadowed Mary meant that he, Michael, disappeared from heaven. By human birth from Mary, the Jewish virgin, he was to become a human soul. This made him available for the fulfillment of Isaiah 53:10 concerning Jehovah's "suffering servant":

"Yet it pleased the LORD to crush him by disease; to see if his soul would offer itself in restitution, that he might see his seed, prolong his days, and that the purpose of the LORD might prosper by his hand."—*JPS;* see also *Zunz.*

EYEWITNESSES TO THE MIRACULOUS BIRTH

21 In due time the surprising pregnancy of the virgin Jewish maiden became manifest to others in Nazareth. Mary's fiancé found it out and was deeply disturbed. Her pregnancy could not be blamed upon him. Ordinary Jewish opinion there in Nazareth would doubt Mary's miraculous conception; the strict Jewish adherents to the Law of Moses would condemn her to be stoned to death as an adulteress that violated her marriage engagement to Joseph. Who could come to Mary's help and save her and her unborn child from death by stoning? Who could clear up things to Joseph? Listen:

"During the time his mother Mary was promised in marriage to Joseph, she was found to be pregnant by holy spirit before they were united. However, Joseph her husband, because he was righteous and did not want to make her a public spectacle, intended to divorce her secretly. But after he had thought these things over, look! Jehovah's angel appeared to him in a dream, saying: 'Joseph, son of David, do not be afraid to take Mary your wife home, for that which has been begotten in her is by holy spirit. She will give birth to a son, and you must call his name Jesus [Hebrew: *Jeshua*], for he will save his people from their sins.'

"All this actually came about for that to be fulfilled which was spoken by Jehovah through his prophet, saying: 'Look! The virgin [according to the Greek *Septuagint*] will become pregnant and will give birth to a son, and they will call his name Immanuel,' which means, when translated, 'With Us Is God.'

"Then Joseph woke up from his sleep and did as the angel of Jehovah had directed him, and he took his wife home. But he had no intercourse with her until she gave birth to a son; and he called his name Jesus [Jeshua]."—Matthew 1:18-25.

21. How was Mary's pregnancy explained to Joseph, and what action then followed?

²² By a comparison of what Gabriel told Mary and what the angel in the dream told Joseph, Gabriel placed the greater emphasis on the role that the Messiah would perform as a King descended from David in order to fulfill Jehovah's covenant with David for an everlasting kingdom. The angel who appeared to Joseph laid the emphasis on the Messiah's role as a priest, as a sin bearer and sin remover. This angel dwelt on the name to be given to the Messiah, the name which, in Hebrew, means "Salvation of Jehovah." The Messiah would live up to his personal name in that he would "save his people from their sins." This agrees with the fact that the Messiah, the Descendant of David, was to become a "priest to time indefinite according to the manner of Melchizedek!"—Psalm 110:1-4.

²³ Did the birth take place in Nazareth after Joseph took Mary to his home there? No, not according to the inspired record. The birth occurred in David's city, Bethlehem of Judah. How so? An imperial decree from Rome worked toward the fulfilling of Micah 5:2, concerning the birthplace of the Messiah. Here is the record:

"Now in those days a decree went forth from Caesar Augustus for all the inhabited earth to be registered; (this first registration took place when Quirinius was governor of Syria;) and all people went traveling to be registered, each one to his own city. Of course, Joseph also went up from Galilee, out of the city of Nazareth, into Judea, to David's city, which is called Bethlehem, because of his being a member of the house and family of David, to get registered with Mary, who had been given him in marriage as promised, at present heavy with child. While they were there, the days came to the full for her to give birth. And she gave birth to her son, the firstborn, and she bound him with cloth bands and laid him in a manger, because there was no place for them in the lodging room."—Luke 2:1-7.

²⁴ The month and the day of birth are not given, even as the birthdays of the people of God are never given in the Holy Bible.

²⁵ With good reason it may be said, however, that Mary's firstborn son Jesus was not born on the fake date of December 25 nor about the time of the winter

---

22. (a) Gabriel, in speaking to Mary, emphasized what feature about her Messianic son? (b) The angel emphasized what other feature about Mary's son to Joseph?
23. How was it that Jesus' birth did not take place in Nazareth?
24, 25. How is the approximate date of Jesus' birth calculated?

festival of *Hhanukkah* (Dedication), which began on the 25th day of the lunar month Kislev. (John 10:22) According to calculations based on Daniel 9:24-27 concerning the appearing, the public career and the cutting off of the Messiah, Jesus was born about the 14th day of the lunar month of Tishri. This was one day before the beginning of the week-long festival of Sukkoth (Booths, Tabernacles), during which festival the Jews would dwell outdoors in booths and the shepherds would be out in the fields guarding their flocks during the watches of the night. (Leviticus 23:34-43; Numbers 29:12-38; Deuteronomy 16:13-16) Since Jesus lived for thirty-three years and a half and he died on Passover day of 33 C.E., or Nisan 14 of that year, this locates his birthday toward the beginning of the autumn of the year 2 B.C.E., or about Tishri 14 of that year.

²⁶ This being the birth of the long-looked-for Messiah, it was too important to let it pass by without eyewitnesses thereto. God saw to it that by sending his angel to announce the miraculous virgin birth. But to whom? To Herod the Great in his royal palace just six miles to the north in Jerusalem? Or to the temple chieftain, High Priest Joazar, who had been appointed by King Herod? Not at all. With security for the newborn child Jesus in mind, Jehovah sent his angel to men who followed the boyhood occupation of David, there in the fields near Bethlehem. He caused no so-called "Star of Bethlehem" to appear for *everybody* to see. We read:

"There were also in that same country shepherds living out of doors and keeping watches in the night over their flocks. And suddenly Jehovah's angel stood by them, and Jehovah's glory gleamed around them, and they became very fearful. But the angel said to them: 'Have no fear, for, look! I am declaring to you good news of a great joy that all the people will have, because there was born to you today a Savior, who is Christ the Lord, in David's city. And this is a sign for you: you will find an infant bound in cloth bands and lying in a manger.' And suddenly there came to be with the angel a multitude of the heavenly army, praising God and saying: 'Glory in the heights above to God, and upon earth peace among men of goodwill.' "—Luke 2:8-14.

²⁷ The angel called the newborn baby lying in a Bethlehem manger a "Savior," which was one of the

---

26. To whom was God's angel sent to announce Jesus' birth, and with what heavenly accompaniment?
27. What terms did the angel apply to the newborn Jesus, and how were they fitting?

reasons why his name was called Jeshua or Jesus, meaning "Salvation of Jehovah." This baby was also to become Jehovah's Anointed One, or Messiah or Christ (Greek). He was also to be "Lord," the One whom even King David speaking prophetically under inspiration called "my Lord."—Psalm 110:1.

[28] Only Almighty God, by a miracle, could provide a child with such an assignment as Messiah. What wonder, then, that an angelic "multitude of the heavenly army" appeared and joined in chanting glory to God! This miraculous birth of all human births was a loving expression of His goodwill toward men whom He approves. Such men having God's goodwill could be at peace in heart and mind. This birth will yet be a reason for "great joy" on the part of "all the people." No wonder that the angelic report of the birth was good news, not alone for heaven, but also for men on earth!

[29] The angel had given to the shepherds the identifying "sign," and so now they could become eyewitnesses to Messiah's birth.

"So when the angels had departed from them into heaven, the shepherds began saying to one another: 'Let us by all means go clear to Bethlehem and see this thing that has taken place, which Jehovah has made known to us.' And they went with haste and found Mary as well as Joseph, and the infant lying in the manger. When they saw it, they made known the saying that had been spoken to them concerning this young child. And all that heard marveled over the things told them by the shepherds, but Mary began to preserve all these sayings, drawing conclusions in her heart. Then the shepherds went back, glorifying and praising God for all the things they heard and saw, just as these had been told them." —Luke 2:15-20.

[30] Thus this miraculous virgin birth is no myth. It has been testified to by heavenly angels, and has been confirmed by human eyewitnesses. The medical doctor Luke made a personal investigation and gathered this vital information for us. (Luke 1:1-4; Colossians 4:14) We are merely hurting ourselves if we do not accept this authentic testimony. We are only keeping ourselves unhappy by high-mindedly rejecting this "good news of a great joy."

28. To whom was glory due on that occasion, and for whom was peace meant, and also "good news of a great joy"?
29. How did the shepherds become eyewitnesses of Messiah's birth?
30. By rejecting this authentic "good news of a great joy," how would we be affecting ourselves?

[31] On the eighth day of his birth the baby was circumcised in the flesh, like all other Jewish boys born under the Law of Moses. (Luke 2:21; Galatians 4:4, 5) At that time, Joseph indicated his adoption of Jesus as his foster child. He adopted no illegitimate child, but protected Jesus against the false charge of being a child of fornication. On the fortieth day of Jesus' birth, Joseph and Mary brought her firstborn son up to Jerusalem to present him at the temple to Jehovah and to have a purification sacrifice made for her and the baby's adoptive father. (Luke 2:22-24; Leviticus 12:1-8) King Herod was not aware of all of this.

[32] In due time Mary had relations with her husband Joseph and bore children to him. The record shows that for at least twelve years after Jesus' birth Joseph continued living with Mary. This allowed for him to have children by her. The record tells of four sons, James, Joseph, Simon and Judas, and also of daughters by Mary. These became half brothers and half sisters to Jesus her firstborn. (Luke 2:41-52; Matthew 13:53-56; Mark 6:1-3; Acts 1:14) However, because Joseph adopted Mary's firstborn son as his own, Joseph passed on to Jesus the legal claim that he had upon the kingdom of David his forefather. Also, by being the natural firstborn of Mary by God's miracle, Jesus inherited a natural claim to the then suspended kingdom of David. In giving the genealogy of his foster-father Joseph, the historian Matthew calls him the Messiah, saying: "The book of the history of Jesus Christ [Hebrew: Messiah], son of David, son of Abraham."—Matthew 1:1. See Luke 3:23-38, showing Mary's lineage.

[33] The birth of Jesus not long before King Herod the Great died was no good news to that Edomite ruler of Jerusalem. He had his attention called to the birth, not by Jehovah's angel or by shepherds of Bethlehem, but by stargazing astrologers from the east, men under demon influence who are condemned in the Law of Moses.—Deuteronomy 18:9-14; Isaiah 47:12-14; Daniel 2:27; 4:7; 5:7.

---

31. When did Joseph adopt Jesus as his foster son and then get purified with the child's mother?
32. (a) Did Mary have other sons and also daughters? (b) The adopted Jesus now had what claims upon the suspended kingdom of David?
33, 34. Why did King Herod not succeed in killing the Messiah, and why did Jesus come to be called "the Nazarene"?

[34] At Herod's court the astrologers had first to have the prophecy of Micah 5:2 pointed out to them before that luminous thing that they imagined was a "star" guided them down to Bethlehem and to where Jesus was housed. God gave them divine warning in a dream not to report back to murderous Herod. Not to be foiled in scheming to kill the Messiah, Herod had the boys two years old and younger in Bethlehem killed, but not Jesus. By angelic warning, Joseph and Mary had taken him down to Egypt. Herod died, leaving his son Archelaus as king of Judea, including Bethlehem. Hence, Jesus was not brought back to Bethlehem but was taken north to Nazareth in Galilee, where he grew up. That is why he came to be called Jesus of Nazareth, not Jesus of Bethlehem.—Matthew 2:1-23; 21:11.

A FORERUNNER INTRODUCES MESSIAH

[35] The Messiah was to be introduced to the nation of Israel by a forerunner, according to the prophecy of Malachi 3:1. (*Leeser; JPS*) This proved to be the son whom the angel Gabriel said would be given to the aged priest Zechariah and his aged wife Elizabeth and whom Zechariah was to call John. (Luke 1:5-25, 57-80) In early spring of the year 29 C.E., during the fifteenth year of the reign of Tiberius Caesar, "God's declaration came to John the son of Zechariah in the wilderness. So he came into all the country around the Jordan, preaching baptism in symbol of repentance for forgiveness of sins." (Luke 3:1-3) He preached to those who came out to hear him, saying: "Repent, for the kingdom of the heavens has drawn near." (Matthew 3:1, 2) This preacher came to be called "John the baptizer."—Mark 1:1-4.

[36] After observing John engaged in preaching and baptizing for about six months, Jesus took action. He recognized that he was to be the earthly representative of that "kingdom of the heavens." By the autumn of that year, 29 C.E., Jesus became thirty years of age. He gave up carpentering there at Nazareth and left his mother there with her other sons and her daughters

---

35. The Messiah was to be introduced by whom, and what did this one preach?
36. When and why did Jesus go to John to get baptized, and what heavenly evidence was given of approval of this?

and went to locate his forerunner, John. He had in
mind the prophetic words of King David as written in
Psalm 40:6-8. (Hebrews 10:1-10) So he went, not to be
baptized in symbol of repentance for forgiveness of
sins, but to be baptized in symbol of presenting himself
to do God's will for him for the future. How did God
show acceptance of him? We read:

"Then Jesus came from Galilee to the Jordan to John, in
order to be baptized by him. But the latter tried to prevent
him, saying: 'I am the one needing to be baptized by you,
and are you coming to me?' In reply Jesus said to him: 'Let
it be, this time, for in that way it is suitable for us to carry
out all that is righteous.' Then he quit preventing him. After
being baptized Jesus immediately came up from the water;
and, look! the heavens were opened up, and he saw descending
like a dove God's spirit coming upon him Look! Also, there
was a voice from the heavens that said: 'This is my Son,
the beloved, whom I have approved.' "—Matthew 3:13-17.

37 John the Baptizer saw what happened and heard
the heavenly Father's voice. Later on he bore witness
to his disciples of what he had seen and had heard
God say from heaven, and he testified, saying: "And
I have seen it, and I have borne witness that this one
is the Son of God." John also pointed to the baptized
Jesus as the one to be sacrificed for the salvation of
mankind, saying: "See, the Lamb of God that takes
away the sin of the world!" (John 1:29-34) Is not John
the Baptizer's testimony worthy of our acceptance and
belief today? Yes, indeed!

38 That descent of God's holy spirit upon the baptized
Jesus meant more than just his becoming henceforth a
spiritual Son of God with his restoration to heavenly
spirit life in view. It also meant his being anointed
with God's spirit. Now in very deed he became the
Anointed One, the Messiah, or, in Greek, the Christ.
Here was the fulfillment of prophecy right on time.
Here, in the year 29 C.E., the seven (year-) weeks and
sixty-two (year-) weeks (a total of 483 years) ended
with the producing of the Anointed One, the Messiah,
the Christ. (Daniel 9:25) Now the seventieth (year-)
week was to begin, at the half point of which the
Messiah would "cause sacrifice and gift offering to

37. What did John testify to his disciples as to who Jesus was,
and how did he refer to him as a sacrificial victim?
38. (a) The descent of God's spirit upon Jesus meant what for
him? (b) What number of "weeks of years" ended there, and
what was to occur during the further week?

cease" by offering his own self as a human sacrifice, he being "cut off" in sacrificial death as the Lamb of God.—Daniel 9:26, 27.

[39] So, too, the prophecy of Isaiah 61:1-3 was fulfilled concerning the anointing of the Messiah with Jehovah's spirit. David had been anointed with mere vegetable oil, but here the Son and Lord of David was anointed with holy spirit. The following year, when Jesus returned to Nazareth, not to do carpentering again, but to preach in their synagogue, he called attention to fulfillment of Isaiah's prophecy in him. The record in Luke 4:16-21 tells us:

"So the scroll of the prophet Isaiah was handed him, and he opened the scroll and found the place where it was written: 'Jehovah's spirit is upon me, because he anointed me to declare good news to the poor, he sent me forth to preach a release to the captives and a recovery of sight to the blind, to send the crushed ones away with a release, to preach Jehovah's acceptable year.' With that he rolled up the scroll, handed it back to the attendant and sat down; and the eyes of all in the synagogue were intently fixed upon him. Then he started to say to them: 'Today this scripture that you just heard is fulfilled.' "

[40] The Great Serpent, Satan the Devil, knew that this anointed Jesus was the Messianic "seed" of God's heavenly "woman." Here, now, of all the "sons of the true God" was the particular one whose integrity the Great Serpent would like to break, to the greatest reproach upon God. So he approached Jesus out in the wilderness of Judea, where Jesus had gone immediately after his baptism and being anointed with Jehovah's spirit, to spend forty days there. The Great Serpent tried to tempt Jesus: To *prove* by a demonstration to the Devil that he was a son of God he should miraculously turn stones into bread or should have the invisible angels carry him on their hands after he had hurled himself down from the battlement of the temple in Jerusalem.

[41] Finally, in a third and last desperate effort, the Tempter offered Jesus "all the kingdoms of the world and their glory" in reward for just one act of worship from Jesus. For a third time Jesus quoted God's written Word and said: "It is written, 'It is Jehovah your

39. Where and on what occasion did Jesus Christ call attention to the fulfillment of Isaiah 61:1-3 in him?
40, 41. (a) Why did Satan want to break especially the integrity of the anointed Jesus? (b) How did the Tempter's testing of Jesus end up?

God you must worship, and it is to him alone you must render sacred service.' "—Matthew 4:1-10.

⁴² The angels were watching this testing of the Messiah's integrity toward the Most High God. So now, when the Devil left in defeat, "look! angels came and began to minister to him." (Matthew 4:11; Mark 1:13) Moses long previously had been forty days with Jehovah's angel up on Mount Horeb in the wilderness of Sinai; and now Jesus the Messiah, after forty days of fasting and meditation in the wilderness of Judea, was ready to enter confidently upon his public career in the land of Israel.—Exodus 24:18.

42. How did Jesus' experience here correspond with Moses' spending forty days on Mount Horeb with God's angel?

CHAPTER 12

The Glorification
of the Messiah

BEFORE the glorification must come the suffering. This was to be the experience of God's Messianic "servant." In foretelling that this was the divine purpose respecting the Messiah, God inspired his prophet Isaiah of the eighth century before our Common Era to say:

"He was oppressed, though he humbled himself and opened not his mouth; as a lamb that is led to the slaughter, and as a sheep that before her shearers is dumb; yea, he opened not his mouth. . . . Therefore will I divide him a portion among the great, and he shall divide the spoil with the mighty; because he bared his soul unto death, and was numbered with the transgressors; yet he bore the sin of many, and made intercession for the transgressors."—Isaiah 53:7-12, *JPS*; Acts 8:32-35.

² Even the forerunner of the Messiah was obliged to suffer for his faithfulness to God's law. After he had

1. What did Jehovah inspire the prophet Isaiah (53:7-12) to say regarding what should precede the glorification of the Messiah?
2. After hearing of John's imprisonment, what message did Jesus take up?

directed many baptized disciples to Jesus, he was imprisoned by the district ruler of Galilee, Herod Antipas, the son of Herod the Great, and later, during a celebration of Herod's birthday, he was beheaded. (Matthew 14:1-12) After Jesus heard of John's arrest and imprisonment, he took up John's message. "From that time on Jesus commenced preaching and saying: 'Repent, you people, for the kingdom of the heavens has drawn near.'"—Matthew 4:12-17.

³ Like John the Baptizer, Jesus was not preaching the earthly kingdom of the Maccabees, which many Jews wanted to be restored. He was preaching the "kingdom of the heavens," the kingdom of God which had a relationship with King David of old. In his suffering he was not unlike the prophet Moses. As regards the strong faith of Moses, it is written in Hebrews 11:25, 26: "Choosing to be ill-treated with the people of God rather than to have the temporary enjoyment of sin, because he esteemed the reproach of the Christ as riches greater than the treasures of Egypt; for he looked intently toward the payment of the reward." Since the Messiah was to be a prophet like Moses, and Moses suffered before and after being appointed (anointed) as Jehovah's prophet, it was but in the proper order of things that the Messiah Jesus should suffer also. In fact, his sufferings should be greater than those of Moses.—Deuteronomy 18:15.

⁴ It was in the name of God Almighty, Jehovah, that Moses was sent back to Egypt to lead his people out of slavery there. (Exodus 3:13-15; 5:22, 23) Just as Moses met with opposition, so his first-century counterpart did. To those who put no faith in him as the Messiah sent from God, Jesus said:

"I have come in the name of my Father, but you do not receive me; if someone else arrived in his own name, you would receive that one. How can you believe, when you are accepting glory from one another and you are not seeking the glory that is from the only God? Do not think that I will accuse you to the Father; there is one that accuses you, Moses, in whom you have put your hope. In fact, if you believed Moses you would believe me, for that one wrote

3. For preferring to be what did Moses suffer, and how should the experience of Jesus correspond with that?
4. In whose name did Moses come to his people, and how does this correspond with the case of Jesus Christ?

about me. But if you do not believe the writings of that one, how will you believe my sayings?"—John 5:43-47.

⁵ We note how Jesus answered those who did not accept him as the Messiah and who said to him: "How long are you to keep our souls in suspense? If you are the Christ [*Ma·shi'ahh*], tell us outspokenly." Jesus asked them to let his Messianic works speak for him, saying: "I told you, and yet you do not believe. The works that I am doing in the name of my Father, these bear witness about me. But you do not believe, because you are none of my sheep. My sheep listen to my voice, and I know them, and they follow me." (John 10:24-27) But there were some Jews that believed that Jesus came in his heavenly Father's name. So, five days before the Passover of 33 C.E., when Jesus, rode into Jerusalem in fulfillment of the prophecy of Zechariah 9:9, a crowd of them hailed him and cried out: "Save, we pray you! Blessed is he that comes in Jehovah's name, even the king of Israel!" —John 12:1, 12, 13; Matthew 21:4-9; Mark 11:7-11; Luke 19:35-38; Psalm 118:26.

⁶ Finally, on Passover night, after celebrating it with his faithful disciples or apostles, Jesus prayed to Jehovah and said:

"I have made your name manifest to the men you gave me out of the world. They were yours, and you gave them to me, and they have observed your word. . . . Holy Father, watch over them on account of your own name which you have given me, in order that they may be one just as we are. When I was with them I used to watch over them on account of your own name which you have given me; and I have kept them."—John 17:6, 11, 12.

So, in coming in Jehovah's name, Jesus was a prophet like Moses.

IDENTIFIED ALSO BY MIRACLES AND PROPHECIES

⁷ Both to the Israelites and to the Egyptians the prophet Moses proved that he came in the name of the one living and true God by means of many miracles. These were God-given "signs" in proof that Jehovah

---

5. Why should the Jews have believed that Jesus came in his heavenly Father's name, and when did a crowd express such a belief?
6. In whose name did Jesus keep watch over his faithful apostles?
7. Why did Moses perform signs before Egyptians and Israelites, and how do his signs compare in number with those of the Messiah?

had sent Moses. (Exodus 4:1-30; 7:1-3; 8:22, 23; 10:1, 2; Deuteronomy 34:10, 11) The ancient Israelites did not demand from Moses a "sign from heaven," and accordingly the Israelites of the first century C.E. were out of order in asking for such a sign from Jesus. (Matthew 16:1-4) It is no discredit to say that the miraculous signs performed by Moses were far outnumbered by those performed by Jesus in proof of his Messiahship.

8 Jesus did not do like Moses and turn water into blood, but he did turn water into the best of wine when supplies ran out at a wedding feast in Cana of Galilee. This was only the start, according to what is written in John 2:11: "Jesus performed this in Cana of Galilee as the beginning of his signs, and he made his glory manifest; and his disciples put their faith in him." As regards the Passover of 30 C.E., the record tells us: "When he was in Jerusalem at the passover, at its festival, many people put their faith in his name, viewing his signs that he was performing." (John 2:23) For example, the Pharisee Nicodemus, a ruler of the Jews and member of the Jerusalem Sanhedrin, visited Jesus by night and said: "Rabbi, we know that you as a teacher have come from God; for no one can perform these signs that you perform unless God is with him." —John 3:1, 2; 7:50, 51; 19:39, 40.

9 Did Moses cure leprosy? Jesus cured many lepers in the land of Israel. Did Moses divide the waters of the Red Sea for the saving of his people? Jesus walked on the waters of the Sea of Galilee and calmed its waters during a dangerous windstorm. Forty years the Israelites lived on manna from heaven in the wilderness and died thereafter. Jesus provided a manna from heaven in the sacrifice of his own perfect humanity, that all those eating of it by faith may live forever. (John 6:48-51) Moses never cured all the cases of sickness and infirmity that Jesus did. Moses never raised anybody from the dead. Jesus raised more persons from the dead than did the prophets Elijah and Elisha, one of these being Lazarus of Bethany, who had been dead and entombed for four days. (John 11:1-45; 12:1-9) Even Jesus' enemies had to admit that he performed many signs, for they said: "What are we to do, because

8. With what did Jesus begin his "signs," and what effect did "signs" have upon his disciples and on Nicodemus?
9. How did Jesus' miracles compare with those of Moses in kind?

this man performs many signs? If we let him alone this way, they will all put faith in him, and the Romans will come and take away both our place and our nation."—John 11:46-48; 12:37.

¹⁰ Without overstating the case, then, the apostle Peter could say to thousands of Jews on the festival day of *Shavuoth* (Weeks) of 33 C.E.: "Men of Israel, hear these words: Jesus the Nazarene, a man publicly shown by God to you through powerful works and portents and signs that God did through him in your midst, just as you yourselves know." (Acts 2:22) Some years later this same Peter, when stating the facts of the case, at Caesarea, to some interested Gentiles who were favorable to the Jews, said:

"You know the subject that was talked about throughout the whole of Judea, starting from Galilee after the baptism that John preached, namely, Jesus who was from Nazareth, how God anointed him with holy spirit and power, and he went through the land doing good and healing all those oppressed by the Devil; because God was with him. And we are witnesses of all the things he did both in the country of the Jews and in Jerusalem."—Acts 10:37-39.

¹¹ Was Moses a prophet? Yes, indeed! And so was the Messiah Jesus. He spoke many prophetic parables or illustrations. He foretold his betrayal by his own apostle Judas and how his own death would occur and by whom, and also that he would be raised from the grave on the third day of his death. He foretold the destruction of Jerusalem, that was to occur at the hands of the Romans in 70 C.E. His most extensive prophecy was that recorded in the accounts preserved in Matthew, chapters twenty-four and twenty-five, Mark, chapter thirteen, and Luke, chapter twenty-one. This prophecy was in answer to the question of his disciples as to when Jerusalem's destruction with its temple would occur, and what would be the "sign" of his Messianic return and "presence" (*parousia*) and that of the "conclusion of the system of things."

¹² In testimony to the accuracy of this prophecy, features of the prophecy were fulfilled during that generation in the first century, and, more remarkably still, corresponding features and other details have been

---

10. How did Peter testify, both to Jews at Pentecost in Jerusalem and to Gentiles in Caesarea, about Jesus' miracles?
11, 12. (a) What is the resemblance of Jesus to Moses as a prophet? (b) What about Jesus' most extensive prophecy as to its undergoing fulfillment?

fulfilled upon our own generation since 1914 C.E., since which year we have had wars, food shortages, earthquakes, pestilences, persecution of his followers, worldwide distress, and an unsurpassed "great tribulation" is ahead.—Matthew 24:21.

¹³ The prophet Moses had no prophecies foretelling him and fulfilled upon him. But in all the Hebrew Scriptures, from Genesis to Malachi, there are hundreds of prophecies that were fulfilled upon Jesus from his birth to his death and resurrection, to prove that he was indeed the Messiah, the "seed" that was to be bruised "in the heel" by the Great Serpent, Satan the Devil. He himself called the attention of his disciples to this after God raised him from the dead. The record in Luke 24:25-48 tells us:

"So he said to them: 'O senseless ones and slow in heart to believe on all the things the prophets spoke! Was it not necessary for the Christ [*Ma·shi'ahh*] to suffer these things and to enter into his glory?' And commencing at Moses and all the Prophets he interpreted to them things pertaining to himself in all the Scriptures. . . .

"He now said to them: 'These are my words which I spoke to you while I was yet with you, that all the things written in the law of Moses and in the Prophets and Psalms about me must be fulfilled.' Then he opened up their minds fully to grasp the meaning of the Scriptures, and he said to them: 'In this way it is written that the Christ [*Ma·shi'ahh*] would suffer and rise from among the dead on the third day, and on the basis of his name repentance for forgiveness of sins would be preached in all the nations—starting out from Jerusalem, you are to be witnesses of these things.' "

¹⁴ In Leviticus, chapter twenty-six, and Deuteronomy 28:15-68 the prophet Moses wrote down all the maledictions and curses that would come upon the nation of Israel for not carrying out their Law covenant with Jehovah God. Moses also wrote:

"And in case there comes to be in a man a sin deserving the sentence of death, and he has been put to death, and you have hung him upon a stake, his dead body should not stay all night on the stake; but you should by all means bury him on that day, because something accursed 'of God is the one hung up; and you must not defile your soil, which Jehovah your God is giving you as an inheritance."—Deuteronomy 21:22, 23.

This law was evidently given by God with his Messiah

---

13. How does Jesus compare with Moses as to having prophecies that foretold him and that were fulfilled upon him?
14. What did Moses write about curses upon Israel and about making a criminal something accursed to God? With whom in view?

in mind. Why? In order for the nation of Israel to be saved from the curse coming upon it for the violating of its Law covenant with God, the Messiah must die on a stake as accursed in place of Israel.

DEATH AND GLORIFICATION

15 On Nisan 14, Passover day, of the year 33 C.E., the Passover lamb was killed and prepared to be eaten, even by Jesus' own apostles. (Matthew 26:1-30; Mark 14:1-26; Luke 22:1-39) But what about the one whom John the Baptist called "the Lamb of God that takes away the sin of the world"? (John 1:29, 36) Late after the Passover supper that night he was betrayed by the apostle Judas Iscariot and was taken into custody by an armed group that took him and turned him over to the religious leaders of Jerusalem. He was put through a trial by the judicial Sanhedrin and sentenced to death according to their interpretation of the Law. In view of their limitations as to the execution of the death penalty, that judicial body turned the condemned Jesus over to the Gentile governor, Pontius Pilate, as a disturber of the peace and a criminal seditionist. The insistence of his accusers was on having him hung upon a stake to die.

16 When on trial before Pontius Pilate, Jesus pointed out that his Messianic kingdom was to be heavenly, not earthly at Jerusalem of the Middle East. When Pilate asked him: "Are you the king of the Jews?" Jesus replied: "My kingdom is no part of this world. If my kingdom were part of this world, my attendants would have fought that I should not be delivered up to the Jews. But, as it is, my kingdom is not from this source." At this answer, Pilate asked: "Well, then, are you a king?" Jesus replied: "You yourself are saying that I am a king. For this I have been born, and for this I have come into the world, that I should bear witness to the truth. Everyone that is on the side of the truth listens to my voice."—John 18:33-37.

17 Unwillingly, Pilate yielded to the demands of the accusers for Jesus to be hung up on a stake. The place

15. On Passover day of 33 C.E., what was done to have the Lamb of God executed by non-Jews?
16. Before Pilate, what did Jesus say about the kingdom and the truth?
17. How was Jesus then 'counted with the transgressors,' and what hope did he impart to one of the transgressors?

of execution proved to be at Golgotha ("Skull Place"), or Calvary, outside the wall of Jerusalem. He was hung up between two criminal evildoers, "transgressors." Those who were versed in the Law of Moses looked upon Jesus upon the stake as "something accursed of God." Although thus "it was with the transgressors that he was counted," Jesus still held in mind the hope of an earthly Paradise for mankind under his future Messianic government. Consequently, when one transgressor, who came to realize that Jesus was an innocent man and a scapegoat for sinners, said to him: "Jesus, remember me when you get into your kingdom," Jesus answered: "Truly I tell you today, You will be with me in Paradise."—Luke 23:39-43; 22:37.

18 About midafternoon of that Passover day, Jesus died. "He bared his soul unto death." "He poured out his soul to the very death." (Isaiah 53:12, JPS; NW) According to Deuteronomy 21:22, 23, he was buried that very afternoon. He was laid in a newly cut tomb belonging to a rich man, in this way making "his burial place even with the wicked ones, and with the rich class in his death, despite the fact that he had done no violence and there was no deception in his mouth." (Isaiah 53:9) Thus, too, Jesus' soul went to Sheol, the common grave of mankind. There it was true of the dead Jesus: "The dead know not anything . . . there is no work, nor device, nor knowledge, nor wisdom, in Sheol, whither thou goest."—Ecclesiastes 9:5, 10, AS; RS.

19 However, King David had written prophetically: "For thou wilt not leave my soul to Sheol; neither wilt thou suffer thy holy one to see corruption. Thou wilt show me the path of life: in thy presence is fullness of joy; in thy right hand there are pleasures for evermore." (Psalm 16:10, 11, AS; RS) True to this prophecy of His own inspiration, Jehovah the Almighty God raised up the Messiah Jesus on the third day, Nisan 16, the day when the high priest Caiaphas at the temple offered up to Jehovah a "sheaf of the firstfruits" of the barley harvest. (Leviticus 23:9-14; 1 Corinthians 15:20, 23) True it was that the tomb in which Jesus

18. How did Jesus make his grave with wicked ones and with the rich ones, and in what condition was he in Sheol?
19. When and how did Jehovah fulfill his own inspired prophecy in Psalm 16:10, and why did a question arise as to Jesus' whereabouts?

had been put was found empty, but why was it that he was nowhere to be found by his own disciples? Why was it that during the forty days after his resurrection he would suddenly appear to them and as suddenly disappear, to prove to them that he was alive from the dead?—Acts 1:1-3; John 20:1-31; Matthew 28:1-18.

[20] The apostle Peter, to whom the resurrected Jesus appeared once privately, gives us the explanation for these materializations such as the spirit angels had made in the days of the ancient prophets. Peter says: "Christ also died for our sins once and for all. He, the just, suffered for the unjust, to bring us to God. In the body he was put to death; in the spirit he was brought to life. And in the spirit he went and made his proclamation to the imprisoned spirits." (1 Peter 3:18, 19, *NEB; RS;* 1 Corinthians 15:5; Luke 24:34) At his resurrection it was done with him as it is foretold to occur to his faithful disciples at their resurrection:

"It is sown in dishonor, it is raised up in glory. It is sown in weakness, it is raised up in power. It is sown a physical body, it is raised up a spiritual body. If there is a physical body, there is also a spiritual one. It is even so written: 'The first man Adam became a living soul.' The last Adam became a life-giving spirit.

"However, this I say, brothers, that flesh and blood cannot inherit God's kingdom, neither does corruption inherit incorruption. . . . For this which is corruptible must put on incorruption, and this which is mortal must put on immortality. But when this which is corruptible puts on incorruption and this which is mortal puts on immortality, then the saying will take place that is written: 'Death is swallowed up forever.' " —1 Corinthians 15:43-45, 50-54.

"For if we have become united with him in the likeness of his death, we shall certainly also be united with him in the likeness of his resurrection."—Romans 6:5.

[21] Accordingly, the Scriptural evidence proves that Jesus Christ was resurrected as a spirit Son of God in immortality and incorruption. (Acts 13:32-37) So, at his resurrection from the dead, Jesus Christ did not withdraw his human body as a sacrifice off God's altar by resuming his human body. (Hebrews 10:1-10) Just as on the annual Day of Atonement the bodies of those animal victims whose blood was taken into the

---

20. How does Peter explain Jesus' resurrection, and how does Paul describe the corresponding resurrection of Jesus' disciples?
21. God resurrected Jesus to be what kind of a person, and so how was it that Jesus retained the merit of his human sacrifice?

Most Holy for sin were disposed of, so God accepted the sacrifice of Jesus' human nature and disposed of Jesus' human body. How? We do not know. (Hebrews 13:10-13; Leviticus, chapter sixteen) Although Almighty God did not resurrect his Son Jesus Christ in a human body, the resurrected Son of God did retain the value or merit of his human sacrifice, which was like the sacrificial blood that the Jewish high priest carried into the Most Holy of the temple so as to make atonement for sin.

²² As a spirit Son of God, Jesus Christ was able to ascend back to heaven on the fortieth day from his resurrection from the dead. A number of his faithful disciples were witnesses to that ascension. (Acts 1:1-11) Just as the Jewish high priest in the Most Holy sprinkled the Atonement blood toward the golden Ark of the Covenant, so Jesus entered into God's heavenly presence and presented the value or merit of his perfect human sacrifice. (Hebrews 9:11-14, 24-26) Then the Most High God seated him at His own right hand as the "priest to time indefinite according to the manner of Melchizedek."—Psalm 110:1-4; Acts 2:31-36; Hebrews 5:10; 10:11-13.

²³ In this way the Son of God was rewarded with a heavenly position higher than the one he held before becoming a perfect man and being bruised "in the heel" by the Great Serpent. He resumed his prehuman name, Michael, so that again there was a "Michael the archangel" in heaven. (Jude 9; Revelation 12:7) The glorified "seed" of God's "woman" was now in a far stronger position to bruise the Serpent's head in God's due time.—Genesis 3:15.

²⁴ How thankful and glad all humanity, natural Jews and Gentiles alike, should be that God's promised Messiah will be a deathless heavenly Messiah, and not a mere earthly human "anointed one" like King David! Under prophetic inspiration, David humbly acknowledged this highly exalted one as his Lord, and this should be our attitude also. We are exhorted to have

22, 23. (a) As a spirit person by resurrection, what was Jesus now able to do as prefigured by the high priest on Atonement Day? (b) How was Jesus now in a stronger position for bruising the Serpent "in the head"?
24, 25. (a) Jews and Gentiles can alike be glad that God's Son is not what kind of a Messiah? (b) In Philippians 2:5-11, what mental attitude are we exhorted to have?

this submissive mental attitude in the following inspired words:

25 "Keep this mental attitude in you that was also in
Christ [Ma·shi'ahh] Jesus, who, although he was existing in God's form, gave no consideration to a seizure,
namely, that he should be equal to God [yet he did not
think to snatch at equality with God, NEB]. No, but
he emptied himself and took a slave's form and came
to be in the likeness of men. More than that, when he
found himself in fashion as a man, he humbled himself
and became obedient as far as death, yes, death on a
torture stake. For this very reason also God exalted
him to a superior position and kindly gave him the
name that is above every other name, so that in the
name of Jesus every knee should bend of those in
heaven and those on earth and those under the ground,
and every tongue should openly acknowledge that
Jesus Christ [Ma·shi'ahh] is Lord to the glory of God
the Father."—Philippians 2:5-11. See also 2 Corinthians
5:16.

CHAPTER 13

Other Mysteries Relative to Messiah Revealed

A MYSTERY has been defined as "any truth un-
knowable except by revelation of God." It is a
"sacred secret" that is revealed by God in his own due
time. (Romans 16:25, 26) For long periods of time
it was a mystery or sacred secret just who would be
the Messiah, the "seed" of God's heavenly "woman."
Also, God's purpose in connection with the Messiah
or Christ was a long-time mystery or sacred secret. But
in his appointed time God revealed, or kept no longer
a secret, that it was his purpose to use the Messiah or
Christ in connection with an administration of all

1, 2. (a) How has the word "mystery" been defined? (b) What
purpose in connection with the Christ has God made an open
secret to us?

things, as in the management of a house by a steward. Such an administration for unity would mean that God would head up all things in the Messiah (Christ) or gather all things together again under the headship of the Messiah or Christ. It was a kindness for God as the Administrator to reveal this, just as we read:

2 "This he caused to abound toward us in all wisdom and good sense, in that he made known to us the sacred secret of his will. It is according to his good pleasure which he purposed in himself for an administration [management as by a steward] at the full limit of the appointed times, namely, to gather all things together again in the Christ [*Ma·shi'ahh*], the things in the heavens and the things on the earth. Yes, in him, in union with whom we [disciples of Christ] were also assigned as heirs, in that we were foreordained according to the purpose [Greek: *pro'-the·sis*] of him who operates all things according to the way his will counsels, that we should serve for the praise of his glory, we who have been first to hope in the Christ."—Ephesians 1:8-12.

3 It was in harmony with this purpose of God that the Messiah Jesus began to lay the foundation for a congregation of which he would be the divinely appointed head. The individual members of this congregation under Christ were not personally foreordained or predestinated; only the number of members and their Christian characteristics were foreordained. Just as he showed by his teachings, Jesus knew that the prophecy of Jeremiah 31:31-34 foretold how Jehovah God would make a "new covenant" with His people. Accordingly, the old Law covenant that Moses had mediated for the natural Jews would come to an end. As it is said in Hebrews 8:13: "In his saying 'a new covenant' he [God] has made the former one obsolete. Now that which is made obsolete and growing old is near to vanishing away." By the time of Jesus' public career that Law covenant of Moses was more than 1,540 years old. And yet after all that time it had failed to produce a "kingdom of priests and a holy nation." (Exodus 19:6) Even down till today, nineteen hundred years later, those natural Jews who claim to be still

---

3. What did God's promise of a "new covenant" mean for the old Mosaic Law covenant and its purpose?

under the Mosaic Law covenant have failed to furnish God with a "kingdom of priests and a holy nation," even their Aaronic priesthood having disappeared since 70 C.E.

⁴ Jesus kept in mind that the nation of Israel was founded upon the twelve patriarchs, the twelve sons of Jacob. (Genesis 49:28) So, from among his disciples, Jesus chose twelve men whom he called "apostles" (sent-forth ones) and who were to be secondary foundations upon him the main foundation of the congregation. (Mark 3:14; Luke 6:13; Ephesians 2:20) Referring to himself as a rock foundation, he said in the hearing of the twelve apostles: "On this rock-mass I will build my congregation, and the gates of Ha'des will not overpower it." (Matthew 16:18) However, down to the day of his death Jesus still recognized the nation of Israel as being the congregation of God, preaching in its synagogues and teaching in its temple at Jerusalem. It was first on the fiftieth day from the day of his resurrection from the dead that the congregation of which he was the head and main foundation was formed. On what basis can that be said? On the following sound basis:

⁵ On that festival day of *Shavuoth* or Pentecost and in fulfillment of the prophecy of Joel 2:28, 29, God's holy spirit was poured out. Upon whom? Upon the nation of Israel that was celebrating its festival of Weeks (*Shavuoth*) there at Jerusalem? No; but upon about one hundred and twenty faithful disciples of Jesus Christ, who were congregated together in an upper chamber in Jerusalem. In visible and audible proof of this, "tongues as if of fire" hovered above their heads and they began speaking with tongues other than their native language. To the thousands of amazed Jews that gathered, the apostle Peter explained that the fulfillment of Joel 2:28, 29 about the outpouring of God's spirit was taking place, and then he added:

"This Jesus God resurrected, of which fact we are all witnesses. Therefore because he was exalted to the right hand of God and received the promised holy spirit from the Father, he has poured out this which you see and hear. Actually

---

4. What is to be said about the foundation of the Christian congregation, and when first was it founded?
5. What was poured out on that festival day of Weeks, and upon whom, and what was Peter's explanation of how it was poured out?

David did not ascend to the heavens, but he himself says, 'Jehovah said to my Lord: "Sit at my right hand, until I place your enemies as a stool for your feet." ' Therefore let all the house of Israel know for a certainty that God made him both Lord and Christ [Ma·shi'ahh], this Jesus whom you impaled."—Acts 2:1-36.

6 Thus, by pouring out holy spirit from God upon his faithful disciples, Jesus was anointing them with holy spirit and was building his congregation. What, then, did this mean for the nation of Israel, that had impaled the Messiah or Christ? It meant that they were no longer the congregation of Jehovah God. It meant that their old Law covenant had vanished away. It had been canceled out, God himself nailing it, as it were, to the stake upon which Jesus Christ had hung as a curse for the nation of Israel on Passover day. (Colossians 2:13, 14; Galatians 3:13) By accepting this Son of God as their sacrificed Messiah, the Jews who were born under that Law covenant could come out from under its curse and receive the blessing of Jehovah God. —Acts 3:25, 26.

7 Moreover, when Jesus Christ presented to his heavenly Father the merit or value of his human lifeblood, he validated a new covenant, the covenant promised in Jeremiah 31:31-34. Just as Moses had mediated the old Law covenant with blood of mere animal sacrifices, so now Jesus Christ in God's presence mediated the new covenant with his own sacrificial blood. In this respect also he was a Prophet like Moses. (Deuteronomy 18:15-18) So a new covenant had replaced the old Law covenant, and the nation of Israel according to the flesh was not in that new covenant. Consequently the nation was no longer the congregation of Jehovah God, no longer the "Israel of God." So all natural Jews born since the cancellation of the Law covenant have never been under that old covenant, even though their rabbis might say they are.

8 With that day of Pentecost of 33 C.E. a spiritual "Israel of God" came into existence, built upon the

---

6. (a) What did Jesus' pouring out the spirit mean as regards his disciples? (b) What did that mean for the nation of Israel and its Law covenant?
7. What did Jesus now mediate by means of his blood, and in what position did this leave the nation of Israel according to the flesh?
8. What kind of Israel came into existence on that day of Pentecost, and how does Peter show the contrast between it and natural Israel?

Messiah Jesus as the rock-mass foundation. "For," as Galatians 6:15, 16 states, "neither is circumcision anything nor is uncircumcision, but a new creation is something. And all those who will walk orderly by this rule of conduct, upon them be peace and mercy, even upon the Israel of God." Showing the contrast between these and the nation that rejected the Messiah Jesus, the apostle Peter wrote to Messiah's disciples: "But you are 'a chosen race, a royal priesthood, a holy nation, a people for special possession, that you should declare abroad the excellencies' of the one that called you out of darkness into his wonderful light."—1 Peter 2:8, 9.

⁹ Not being under the old Mosaic Law covenant, this spiritual "Israel of God" does not celebrate the annual Passover. On finishing the last Passover that Jesus celebrated with his apostles in Jerusalem, Jesus took a loaf of unleavened bread and a cup of wine and started a new annual supper for his followers in memorial of his own death as the Lamb of God and as the Mediator of the new covenant. After saying a blessing over the cup of wine, he said to his faithful apostles: "Drink out of it, all of you; for this means my 'blood of the covenant,' which is to be poured out in behalf of many for forgiveness of sins." (Matthew 26:27, 28; compare with Exodus 24:8.) But of what covenant was Jesus talking? Luke's account of Jesus' words tells us, saying: "This cup means the new covenant by virtue of my blood, which is to be poured out in your behalf."—Luke 22:20; 1 Corinthians 11:20-26.

¹⁰ It was the "new covenant" as foretold in Jeremiah 31:31-34 that Jesus' blood was to validate, to bring about God's forgiveness of the sins of thos taken into the new covenant. This new covenant Jesus validated when he presented the value or merit of his blood to Jehovah God after ascending to heaven. By virtue of this he became the Mediator of the new covenant, which was a better covenant than that mediated by Moses at Mount Sinai in 1513 B.C.E. (Hebrews 8:6-13; 9:15-20; 12:24; 13:20; 1 Timothy 2:5, 6) Un-

---

9. What new supper did Jesus start for his disciples, and of what covenant did he speak?
10. How did that covenant compare with the one mediated by Moses, and why were certain natural, circumcised Jews not taken into that new covenant?

happily, the natural, circumcised Jews that refused to accept Jesus as the Messiah were not taken into the new covenant and hence did not become part of the spiritual "Israel of God."

[11] After Jesus had his apostles drink the cup of wine that represented his blood that was to be applied to the new covenant, he continued talking to them and said: "You are the ones that have stuck with me in my trials; and I make a covenant with you, just as my Father has made a covenant with me, for a kingdom, that you may eat and drink at my table in my kingdom, and sit on thrones to judge the twelve tribes of Israel." (Luke 22:28-30) This was an assurance that the new covenant validated by Jesus' blood would be successful in producing a "kingdom of priests and a holy nation." The faithful members of the spiritual "Israel of God" who are taken into the new covenant will share with Jesus Christ in the heavenly kingdom that would rule over more than the earthly territory of King David. These will also serve as underpriests of the Lord Jesus Christ, who was to be made a "priest to time indefinite according to the manner of Melchizedek!"—Psalm 110:4.

MYSTERY RELATIVE TO ABRAHAM'S "SEED" UNLOCKED

[12] Since God's covenant promise to the patriarch Abraham back in 1943 B.C.E., the mystery existed, Of whom will the promised "seed" of Abraham be composed, for the blessing of all the families of the ground? (Genesis 12:1-3) On the day of Pentecost of 33 C.E., this mystery was unlocked. The "seed" was to be composed of more than just the Messiah Jesus, of course, for God had promised Abraham that his seed would be like the stars of the heavens and the grains of sand on the seashore. Natural, circumcised Israel did become like that, but Abraham's true seed was to be composed, not of natural Israel according to the flesh, but of spiritual Israel, who are begotten by God's spirit to become spiritual sons of God with a

11. At the new supper, what did Jesus say to his apostles about a kingdom, and what success did this assure for the new covenant?
12. On Pentecost of 33 C.E., what mystery was unlocked regarding the "seed" of Abraham, and what kind of "seed" was it to be?

heavenly inheritance in view. God is the Greater Abraham, the name meaning "Father of a Multitude."

[13] However, the people of natural Israel were given the first opportunity to become the members of the spiritual "seed" of Abraham. On the day of Pentecost of 33 C.E. it was natural, circumcised Jews, natural descendants of Abraham, that were begotten by God's holy spirit as His sons and taken into the new covenant. Thereby Jehovah God became the Greater Abraham to this spiritual "seed." Although the nation of Israel had shared in cutting off the Messiah in death at the half of the 'seventieth week of years' (from 29 to 36 C.E.), yet Jehovah God continued showing them favor for the latter half of that seventieth week of years out of regard for his covenant with Abraham, whose fleshly descendants the nation of Israel was. (Daniel 9:24-27) So the opportunity to become Abraham's spiritual "seed" continued to be offered first to them to the end of the seventieth week.

[14] Some days after Pentecost the apostle Peter pointed out this kindly provision of God, when speaking to a crowd of Jews at the Jerusalem temple: "And all the prophets, in fact, from Samuel on and those in succession, just as many as have spoken, have also plainly declared these days. You are the sons of the prophets and of the covenant which God covenanted with your forefathers, saying to Abraham, 'And in your seed all the families of the earth will be blessed.' To you first God, after raising up his Servant, sent him forth to bless you by turning each one away from your wicked deeds."—Acts 3:24-26.

[15] Some years later a former Pharisee, who used to be very zealous for the Jewish traditions, wrote the following words:

"Christ [Ma·shi'ahh] by purchase released us from the curse of the Law by becoming a curse instead of us, because it is written: 'Accursed is every man hanged upon a stake.' The purpose was that the blessing of Abraham might come to be by means of Jesus Christ for the nations, that we might receive the promised spirit through our faith."

---

13. On Pentecost, to whom was the opportunity given to become part of the spiritual "seed" of Abraham, and for how long was this opportunity held out to them exclusively, and why?
14. How did Peter, at the Jerusalem temple, point out this kindly provision for the natural seed of Abraham?
15. To whom, then, did the blessing of Abraham's "seed" come first, and how were the blessed ones released from slavery?

"But when the full limit of the time arrived, God sent forth his Son, who came to be out of a woman and who came to be under law, that he might release by purchase those under law, that we, in turn, might receive the adoption as sons. Now because you are sons, God has sent forth the spirit of his Son into our hearts and it cries out: 'Abba, Father!' So, then, you are no longer a slave but a son; and if a son, also an heir through God."—Galatians 3:13, 14; 4:4-7.

16 Explaining that membership in the "seed of Abraham" is based not on a fleshly connection with Abraham but on exercising such faith as Abraham had, the foregoing writer, the apostle Paul, said: "Surely you know that those who adhere to faith are the ones who are sons of Abraham. Now the Scripture, seeing in advance that God would declare people of the nations righteous due to faith, declared the good news beforehand to Abraham, namely: 'By means of you all the nations will be blessed.' You are all, in fact, sons of God through your faith in Christ Jesus. For all of you who were baptized into Christ have put on Christ. There is neither Jew nor Greek, there is neither slave nor freeman, there is neither male nor female; for you are all one person in union with Christ Jesus. Moreover, if you belong to Christ, you are really Abraham's seed, heirs with reference to a promise."—Galatians 3:7, 8, 26-29; Genesis 12:3.

A MYSTERY UNLOCKED GENERATIONS LATER

17 Not all fleshly descendants of Abraham had the faith that he had and that resulted in his being called righteous and the "friend" of God even before he was circumcised in the flesh. (Genesis 15:6; Romans 4:9-12; James 2:21-23) So not many of the natural Jews took advantage of the 'seventieth week of years' during which the Abrahamic covenant was 'kept in force' in behalf of the fleshly descendants of Abraham, Isaac and Jacob. (Daniel 9:27) Only a small remnant did so. The latest figure for those Jews at Jerusalem who accepted the Messiah Jesus before the end of the 'seventieth week of years' in 36 C.E. was given as about five thousand.—Acts 4:4.

---

16. One's being a member in the spiritual "seed" of Abraham is based upon a fleshly connection, or upon what?
17. How many Jews had faith like that of Abraham and took advantage of the 'seventieth week of years' of divine favor to them?

¹⁸ God had foreordained a number far larger than that for his "kingdom of priests and a holy nation" that was to be produced by the new covenant. The exact number that he purposed to have he did not reveal till after Jerusalem was destroyed in 70 C.E. and toward the end of the first century. Then to the aged surviving apostle John he revealed the purposed chosen number of spiritual Israelites to be 144,000. (Revelation 7:4-8; 14:1-3) When the 'seventieth week' ended in the autumn of 36 C.E., the number of Jews who had accepted Jesus as Messiah and who had been baptized with holy spirit was evidently far less than 144,000. What then? Had God's purpose failed? Or, what surprising step would he now take toward not letting his "eternal purpose" in Christ fail?

¹⁹ Down till the autumn of 36 C.E. the congregation of the baptized followers of the Messiah Jesus consisted exclusively of natural Jews, circumcised Samaritans and others who had become circumcised proselytes of the Jewish faith. (Acts 2:10; 8:1 through 9:30; 11:19) The rest of mankind were unbelievers, "without Christ, alienated from the state of Israel and strangers to the covenants of the promise," having "no hope" and being "without God in the world." (Ephesians 2:11, 12) Now came a revelation: The body of believers under the Messiah Jesus as their Head was no longer to be exclusively of persons drawn from the Jewish race and Jewish proselytes. Henceforth there were to be taken into the body of Messianists uncircumcised believers, persons just as uncircumcised as Abraham was when God called him and then made the covenant with him and justified him to friendship with God because of faith. So, too, these accepted non-Jews had faith.

²⁰ In the middle of the 'seventieth week' in 33 C.E., God had abolished the Mosaic Law covenant and had inaugurated the better "new covenant" with spiritual Israel. So the old Law covenant should no longer stand as a barrier between Jew and Gentile. So, mov-

---

18. How many did God purpose to have of the spiritual Israelites, and so what questions arose at the end of the 'seventieth week'?
19. What revelation did God now make regarding the body of baptized believers under the Messiah Jesus as Head?
20. (a) So what was no longer to stand as a barrier between Jew and non-Jew? (b) So to whom did God now turn favorable attention?

ing down a cleared path, as stated in Ephesians 2:13-18, Jehovah God turned his attention favorably to the uncircumcised Gentile nations in order "to take out of them a people for his name."—Acts 15:14; Amos 9:11, 12, Greek *Septuagint Version*.

21 At the end of the seventieth week of years, Jehovah God sent his angel, to whom? To an uncircumcised Gentile at the capital city of the Roman governor over the province of Judea. Cornelius was this Gentile man, a centurion of the Italian band, but "a devout man and one fearing God together with all his household, and he made many gifts of mercy to the people and made supplication to God continually." Cornelius was told to send to the south to the seacoast city of Joppa and have Simon Peter brought up from there. Simon Peter went along with the three men who were sent to get him, he having been instructed to go along with them and to "stop calling defiled the things God has cleansed."

22 So smothering his prejudice against entering a Gentile home, Simon Peter went in to Cornelius' home at Caesarea. On invitation he preached to this Gentile and those whom he had gathered into his house to hear the apostle Peter. Peter preached to them about the Messiah whom God had sent to Israel. "Also," Peter continued on to say, "he ordered us to preach to the people and to give a thorough witness that this is the One decreed by God to be judge of the living and the dead. To him all the prophets bear witness, that everyone putting faith in him gets forgiveness of sins through his name."—Acts 10:1-43; 11:4-14.

23 Those words were enough for Cornelius and those listening with him. Also, God read their hearts and took action. We read:

"While Peter was yet speaking about these matters the holy spirit fell upon all those hearing the word. And the faithful ones that had come with Peter [six circumcised Jewish believers] who were of those circumcised were amazed, because the free gift of the holy spirit was being poured out also upon people of the nations. For they heard them speaking with tongues and [magnifying] God. Then Peter responded:

21. To whom did God then send his angel, and what did this one do?
22. In the Gentile home, what did Peter preach about to the gathering and say about forgiveness of sins?
23. At what miracle did Peter command his listeners to be baptized, and in whose name?

'Can anyone forbid water so that these might not be baptized who have received the holy spirit even as we have?' With that he commanded them to be baptized in the name of Jesus Christ. Then they requested him to remain for some days."—Acts 10:44-48; 11:1-17.

24 Later, on his return to Jerusalem, Peter explained to the circumcised Jewish believers there his course, saying: "If, therefore, God gave the same free gift to them as he also did to us who have believed upon the Lord Jesus Christ, who was I that I should be able to hinder God?" We today should be like those back there who heard Peter's explanation: "Now when they heard these things, they acquiesced, and they glorified God, saying: 'Well, then, God has granted repentance for the purpose of life to people of the nations also.'"—Acts 11:17, 18.

25 From then on, the apostles and fellow Jewish believers did not restrict themselves only to Jews and proselytes, but did what the resurrected Jesus told them to do: "Go therefore and make disciples"—of whom?—"of people of all the nations, baptizing them in the name of the Father and of the Son and of the holy spirit, teaching them to observe all the things I have commanded you. And, look! I am with you all the days until the conclusion of the system of things."—Matthew 28:19, 20.

26 Prior to the conversion of Cornelius to discipleship of the Messiah, Saul of Tarsus, who had been a conscientious persecutor of Messianic believers of his own Jewish people, himself got converted. He promptly started preaching to other circumcised Jews, showing them from the inspired Hebrew Scriptures that this Jesus, the son of David, was the foretold Messiah or Christ. In course of time he was given the standing of an apostle and was called Paul, and was specially made "an apostle to the nations." He in particular wrote about what a marvelous mystery, or "sacred secret," it was that God revealed there in 36 C.E. by His admitting of believing Gentiles into the body of Christ's disciples, as members of the "seed of Abraham."—Romans 11:13.

24. What did those Jews in Jerusalem who heard Peter's explanation do in response?
25. What command of the resurrected Jesus did the circumcised Jewish believers then obey?
26. What apostle in particular wrote about God's mystery with reference to believing Gentiles?

²⁷ For example, Paul wrote concerning the long-secret feature of the Messianic congregation: "I became a minister of this congregation in accordance with the stewardship from God which was given me in your interest to preach the word of God fully, the sacred secret [or, the mystery] that was hidden from the past systems of things and from the past generations. But now it has been made manifest to his holy ones, to whom God has been pleased to make known what are the glorious riches of this sacred secret among the nations. It is Christ in union with you, the hope of his glory." (Colossians 1:25-27) What a grand "sacred secret," to be revealed after such long periods of time, that believers from among the Gentile nations should be given the heavenly "hope" of being glorified with the Messiah, Christ! It was indeed an honor and a privilege to be a minister of a congregation with such a hope!

²⁸ O just to think that all this loving consideration is within the lofty purpose that God formed in connection with his Messiah, so as to make Gentile believers part of the spiritual "seed" of Abraham for blessing all mankind! How admirable it is that the loving God has stuck to this generous feature of his will, because it is part of his "eternal purpose"! In expressing appreciation for his own God-given part in this connection, Paul says:

²⁹ "To me, a man less than the least of all holy ones, this undeserved kindness was given, that I should declare to the nations the good news about the unfathomable riches of the Christ and should make men see how the sacred secret is administered which has from the indefinite past been hidden in God, who created all things. This [procedure] was to the end that now to the governments and the authorities in the heavenly places there might be made known through the congregation the greatly diversified wisdom of God, according to the eternal purpose [Greek: *pro'the·sis*] that he formed in connection with the Christ, Jesus our Lord."—Ephesians 3:8-11.

---

27. What grand "sacred secret" was Paul making known among the Gentile nations?
28, 29. (a) This loving consideration for Gentile believers was contained in God's purpose in connection with whom? (b) In expressing gratitude for his part in this connection, what did Paul write about God's "eternal purpose"?

³⁰ Thus God proceeded in such a way with his "sacred secret" that, "according to the eternal purpose that he formed in connection with the Christ," there might now at this time be made manifest to the governments and the authorities in the heavenly places the "greatly diversified wisdom of God" by the producing of the Christian congregation as an example thereof. Are we not highly favored to be living in this time of understanding the "sacred secret" of God according to his "eternal purpose"? Paul says:

"In other generations this secret was not made known to the sons of men as it has now been revealed to his holy apostles and prophets by spirit, namely, that people of the nations should be joint heirs and fellow members of the body and partakers with us of the promise in union with Christ Jesus through the good news."—Ephesians 3:5, 6.

³¹ Ancient pre-Christian prophets, yes, even angels, were interested in just how this "sacred secret" would be administered by Jehovah God.

"Concerning this very salvation a diligent inquiry and a careful search were made by the prophets who prophesied about the undeserved kindness meant for you. They kept on investigating what particular season or what sort of season the spirit in them was indicating concerning Christ when it was bearing witness beforehand about the sufferings [destined, in store] for Christ and about the glories to follow these. It was revealed to them that, not to themselves, but to you, they were ministering the things that have now been announced to you through those who have declared the good news to you with holy spirit sent forth from heaven. Into these very things angels are desiring to peer."—1 Peter 1:10-12, NW; An American Translation.

³² So in God's due time it was revealed that the full membership of Christ's "body" would be made up of Gentiles as well as Jews. God's "eternal purpose," as first formed at the Garden of Eden, took into account this congregation having the Messiah as its Head. In it both Jews and Gentiles were unified.

---

30. (a) According to His "eternal purpose," how did God proceed to make manifest his "greatly diversified wisdom"? (b) Why are we highly favored to be living at this time?
31, 32. (a) Who in pre-Christian times were interested in understanding these things? (b) So from whom will Christ's "body" be made up?

CHAPTER 14

Triumph for
the "Eternal Purpose"

GOD'S "eternal purpose" has its opposers in heaven and on earth. They have fought and still keep on fighting to prevent the ultimate triumph of that "eternal purpose." When at the Garden of Eden God announced his "eternal purpose" in the hearing of the Great Serpent and of the sinful Adam and Eve, God said to the Serpent: "And I shall put enmity between you and the woman and between your seed and her seed. He will bruise you in the head and you will bruise him in the heel." (Genesis 3:15) Since then Satan the Devil and those disobedient angels who have become demons have unitedly fought against God's stated purpose.

² After the spiritual "Israel of God" was founded on its twelve apostolic foundations on the festival day of Pentecost of 33 C.E., there were devilish attempts made on earth to destroy this newly created "chosen race," this "royal priesthood," this "holy nation." (1 Peter 2:9) First, violent persecution was used, but failed. (Acts 7:59 through 8:4; 9:1-5, 21; 11:19) Then the corrupting of spiritual Israel in its teachings and way of life was attempted, and it wrought great havoc. The apostle Peter, writing to upholders of the Christian faith about the year 64 C.E., forewarned the first-century Christians of this coming invasion of spiritual corruption, saying:

"Prophecy was at no time brought by man's will, but men spoke from God as they were borne along by holy spirit. However, there also came to be false prophets among the people, as there will also be false teachers among you. These very ones will quietly bring in destructive sects and will disown even the owner that bought them, bringing speedy destruction upon themselves. Furthermore, many will follow their acts of

1. Who have been spirit opposers of God's "eternal purpose," and since when?
2. (a) By what means were devilish attempts made to destroy the newly created "chosen race"? (b) What did Peter write in warning against the invasion by corruptive elements?

loose conduct, and on account of these the way of the truth will be spoken of abusively. Also, with covetousness they will exploit you with counterfeit words. But as for them, the judgment from of old is not moving slowly, and the destruction of them is not slumbering."—2 Peter 1:21 through 2:3; see also Jude 4.

3 Likewise, the apostle Paul, when on his last journey to Jerusalem, warned the elders of the Christian congregation: "I know that after my going away oppressive wolves will enter in among you and will not treat the flock with tenderness, and from among you yourselves men will rise and speak twisted things to draw away the disciples after themselves." (Acts 20:29, 30) Also, in a letter written earlier to the congregation in Thessalonica, Macedonia, he gave a warning of the breaking out of a religious rebellion in the congregation and of the revealing of the "man of lawlessness," "the son of destruction." Paul warned that "the mystery of this lawlessness is already at work." This "lawless one" was to be a composite person, the clergy class of Christendom. (2 Thessalonians 2:3-9) This composite "man of lawlessness" was revealed in the fourth century C.E., when the Roman emperor, Constantine the Great, dealt with corrupt "bishops" and made their religion the state religion for the Roman Empire. Constantine set up an official clergy class. Thus Christendom came to be.

4 For the next sixteen centuries, down into this twentieth century, what kind of record has Christendom made for herself? A record of her clergymen involving themselves in politics, introducing more and more pagan teachings into their religious faith, accumulating wealth and power for themselves, oppressing their religious flocks, fomenting religious wars, cruel crusades and persecutions, establishing hundreds of confusing sects, blessing the armies of so-called "Christian" nations that were at war with one another, corrupting the morals of their church members, hiding God's "eternal purpose" and really working against it, just like the earthly, visible "seed" of the Great Serpent. There was no real Christian unity within

3. (a) How did Paul warn against corrupters of the congregation? (b) Who is the "man of lawlessness," and when was this one revealed?
4. During the centuries since her founding, what record has Christendom's clergy made for itself, and yet what does Christendom claim to be?

her. There were enormous stains of bloodguilt on her religious skirts. No cultivating of the fruits of God's holy spirit within her, especially brotherly love! Rather, the "works of the flesh" abounded in her. (John 13:34, 35; Galatians 5:19-24) And yet, in spite of the condemning Bible evidence against her, she claimed to be the "Israel of God."

5 Did all this misrepresenting of God and of his spiritual Israel block Him from successfully carrying out His "eternal purpose"? Not for a minute! He had foreseen all of this and had foretold it in his written Word, the Holy Bible. His new covenant with spiritual Israel continued in force, and, without doubt, he kept on selecting and preparing spiritual Israelites for a share with the Messiah Jesus in the promised heavenly kingdom.

6 Since the number of spiritual Israelites who are sealed for joint heirship with the Messiah in the heavenly kingdom is limited to 144,000, according to Revelation 7:4-8; 14:1-3, the time must come when the last ones needed to complete the full number of the Kingdom class would be found here on earth. Instead of being religiously divided like the religious sects of Christendom, they would be gathered together into a spiritual unity in spite of race, color, nationality or tribal ties. As they are no part of this world, they would be harvested out from this world.—John 17:14-23.

7 The Lord Jesus, when explaining to his apostles the mysteries or "sacred secrets of the kingdom," spoke of this final gathering of these "sons of the kingdom" as being a "harvest." He indicated when this spiritual "harvest" would take place, when he said:

"The harvest is a conclusion of a system of things, and the reapers are angels. Therefore, just as the weeds are collected and burned with fire, so it will be in the conclusion of the system of things. The Son of man will send forth his angels, and they will collect out from his kingdom all things that cause stumbling and persons who are doing lawlessness, and they will pitch them into the fiery furnace. There is where their weeping and the gnashing of their teeth will be. At that time the righteous ones will shine as brightly as the sun in the

5. Despite misrepresentation by Christendom, what has God been doing according to his "eternal purpose"?
6. Into what condition would the last ones of the 144,000 on earth be brought?
7. To what did Jesus liken that gathering work, and where did he locate it?

kingdom of their Father. Let him that has ears listen."
—Matthew 13:11, 39-43.

8 At that "conclusion of the system of things" other
things were foretold to happen besides this harvesting
of the "sons of the kingdom." (Matthew 24:31) All
these other things together with the spiritual harvest
would be earmarks to identify the time in which we
are living, that it is the foretold "conclusion of the
system of things." The Messiah Jesus, the prophet like
Moses, enumerated these things in answer to the question of his apostles directly after he had foretold the
destruction of the temple of Jerusalem. They asked
him: "When will these things be, and what will be
the sign of your presence [Greek: *parousia*] and of
the conclusion of the system of things?"—Matthew
23:37 through 24:3.

9 In the account in Matthew 24:4-22 we can read how,
in answer, Jesus predicted again the destruction of
Jerusalem, also the wars, famines, earthquakes, persecution upon his faithful disciples, increasing lawlessness and cooling off of love, preaching activity by his
disciples, and their flight from Judea and Jerusalem
after seeing the holy place desecrated by the "disgust-
ing thing that causes desolation." This was to occur
within "this generation" of which he and his apostles
were a part. This meant that Jerusalem and the
system of things based upon it as a national religious
center were in their "time of the end." That "time of
the end" began in the year 29 C.E., when John the
Baptizer began preaching, "Repent, for the kingdom
of the heavens has drawn near," and then baptized
Jesus, and it ended in the year 70 C.E. with the des-
olating of Jerusalem and its temple and the disap-
pearance of the Aaronic priesthood. Jewry and Judaism
have never been the same since.

THE SIGN OF THE "TIME OF THE END"

10 However, Jesus spoke of many things to happen
after Jerusalem was destroyed, adding: "And Jerusa-

---

8. Was this spiritual "harvest" the only thing to happen during
the "conclusion of the system of things," and in reply to what
question did Jesus furnish the answer?
9. What did Jesus predict for then, and when did Jerusalem's
"time of the end" begin and conclude?
10. In his prophecy, how did Jesus use first-century Jerusalem,
so that his prophecy applies today?

lem will be trampled on by the nations, until the appointed times of the nations are fulfilled." (Luke 21: 20-24) It is evident, after careful study of Jesus' complete prophecy, as found in Matthew, chapters twenty-four and twenty-five, Mark, chapter thirteen, and Luke, chapter twenty-one, that Jesus was also using first-century Jerusalem as a prophetic picture of its modern-day counterpart, Christendom, and the system of things that obtained among the Jews scattered world wide as a picture of the present-day worldwide system of things, dominated by Christendom. So Jesus' prophecy on the "conclusion of the system of things" applies also today, for its complete fulfillment. Why do we say "today"? Do we mean that we today are living in the foretold "conclusion of the system of things"? Yes!

11 The world today is living in its "time of the end." Let us remember how, when that "ancient world," the "world of ungodly people," "the world of that time," of Noah's time, was deluged with a global flood, its "time of the end" began one hundred and twenty years before the watery cataclysm of 2370 B.C.E. (2 Peter 2:5; 3:6; Genesis 6:1-3; Matthew 24:37-39) Before the destruction of Jerusalem in 607 B.C.E. by the Babylonians, God spoke to the last Davidic king on the throne of Jerusalem, Zedekiah, and referred to the "time of the error of the end." Jerusalem's "time of the end" was then forty years long, beginning when God raised up Jeremiah to be his prophet in the thirteenth year of the reign of Josiah. (Ezekiel 21:25; Jeremiah 1:1, 2; Ezekiel 4:6, 7) Jerusalem of the first century C.E. also had its "time of the end," of forty-one years (29-70 C.E.).—Luke 19:41-44; 1 Thessalonians 2:16.

12 Many years after the first destruction of Jerusalem by the Babylonians, God's angel spoke to the prophet Daniel about the "time of the end" that was to come upon the worldwide system of things. (Daniel 11:35 through 12:4) We have been in that "time of the end" since the year 1914 C.E. We say this, not just because in that year World War I burst forth

---

11. In what period of time does this world find itself, this corresponding with what previous similar periods?
12. Jehovah used what prophet to mention the "time of the end," and what, since 1914 C.E., shows we are in that period?

and introduced an age of violence and war potential that threatens the wiping out of the entire human race. It is true also that since that momentous year Jesus' prophecy concerning the "sign" of the conclusion of the system of things has been undergoing a complete fulfillment. And since this "conclusion of the system of things" will culminate in what Jesus called "great tribulation such as has not occurred since the world's beginning until now, no, nor will occur again," it means that we are nearing the complete end of this system of things, and with it the destruction of a "world of ungodly people."—Matthew 24:21.

13 Yet, the reason why the year 1914 C.E. is to be fixed upon is that in that year the "presence" (*parousia*) of the Lord Jesus in Messianic kingdom authority began. That his invisible "presence" was true in this respect is indicated by a particular thing that he said in answering the apostles' question about the "sign of your presence." It was this, as recorded in Matthew 24:14: "And this good news of the kingdom will be preached in all the inhabited earth for a witness to all the nations; and then the end will come." In answering his apostles, Jesus gave no date, and yet the unfolding of the "sign" from the year 1914 forward till now seals that year as the time of the birth of God's Messianic kingdom in the hands of his Son Jesus Christ in the heavens. But there is another way of arriving at that date to verify that it is the foreordained time for the Kingdom's birth with Christ's "presence" in it. What is that other way of verifying 1914?

14 In his prophecy as to "When will these things be?" he foretold the impending destruction of Jerusalem and added: "And Jerusalem will be trampled on by the nations, until the appointed times of the nations are fulfilled." (Luke 21:20-24) Those "appointed times of the [non-Jewish, Gentile] nations" began back in 607 B.C.E. when the Babylonians destroyed Jerusalem and overthrew the reigning descendant of King David, the heir of the divine covenant for an everlasting kingdom. These Gentile Times, as they are often called, continued

---

13. (a) How does Matthew 24:14 show that Christ's "presence" was to be in connection with God's kingdom? (b) Since Christ gave no date, what problem arises?
14. When did the Gentile Times mentioned by Jesus begin, and past what event were they to continue?

on down to Jesus' day and were to continue on after the second destruction of the holy city. It is a fact that after seventy years of desolation of Jerusalem and the land of Judah a faithful remnant of the Jews returned from exile in the land of Babylon and rebuilt Jerusalem and other cities in the long-desolated land. But that did not mean that Jerusalem had ceased to be trampled on by the Gentile nations, first by the Babylonians and next by the Medo-Persians who conquered Babylon.

¹⁵ Why not? Because, with the rebuilding of Jerusalem from 537 B.C.E. forward, the throne and Messianic kingdom of the royal line of David were not restored to Jerusalem. Jerusalem was now in a province of the Medo-Persian Empire and was under the domination of Darius the Mede and Cyrus the Great, the Persian. So what Jerusalem had stood for since its capture by King David in the year 1070 B.C.E. was still trampled on, namely, Jerusalem's rank as capital of the Messianic kingdom of the sons and successors of King David. The Maccabean kingdom of Levite rulers (104-63 and 40-37 B.C.E.) did not alter that fact. Then, when Jesus the "son of David" came and presented himself as the one anointed with God's spirit, the majority of the Jewish religious leaders and their followers did not want him as their Messiah and King. They cried out to the Roman Governor Pontius Pilate: "We have no king but Caesar." (John 19:15) So onward the Gentile Times marched, and the right to Messianic kingship was trampled on still further.

¹⁶ However, Jesus said: "Until the appointed times of the nations are fulfilled." How long after Babylon overturned the throne of King David at Jerusalem in 607 B.C.E. were those times of Gentile interference with God's Messianic kingdom to continue?

¹⁷ Now, of course, after seeing what has happened in fulfillment of Jesus' prophecy since World War I broke out, we can confidently answer, Until the fulfillment of the Gentile Times in 1914 C.E. Yes, but, more than that, in the days of King Nebuchadnezzar,

---

15. (a) Why did the Gentile Times continue on after Jerusalem was rebuilt in 537 B.C.E.? (b) Why did those Times continue on after Jesus' trial before Pontius Pilate?
16, 17. (a) Because of fulfillment of Jesus' prophecy, we say that the Gentile Times were fulfilled when? (b) To what ancient king did God reveal the time length, and how had God used this king?

who destroyed Jerusalem in 607 B.C.E., God revealed that he had marked off how long those Gentile Times as then beginning would run without interference from the Messianic kingdom of God. God indicated that it would be for seven symbolic "times." The dream in which God revealed this time period to Nebuchadnezzar was interpreted by the prophet Daniel. (Daniel 4:16, 23, 25, 32) God used Nebuchadnezzar like a woodcutter to chop down the earthly expression of God's kingdom at Jerusalem in 607 B.C.E. The stump of that symbolic "tree" was to be banded and not allowed to sprout and produce a new tree until after the end of "seven times."

18 In the meantime, during those "seven times," the Gentile world rulers would exercise the rulership that really belonged to the royal line of King David due to God's covenant with him for an everlasting kingdom. But those Gentile rulers wielded that power of rulership in a very untheocratic way, in an anti-Messianic way, as with an unreasonableness like that displayed by Nebuchadnezzar during his seven years of madness. But just as a sane Nebuchadnezzar was restored to rulership at the end of those seven years, so the Messianic feature of God's kingdom was to be restored at the close of the "seven times" of Gentile world domination. Then the royal stump was to be unbanded, and from its roots a new tree of rulership was to grow up. —Daniel 4:1-37.

19 Now if we measure back from 1914 C.E. to 607 B.C.E., it amounts to 2,520 years. If, next, we take the number of the "times," seven, and divide it into 2,520 years, it results in 360 years. That is the length of a prophetic "time" in the Holy Scriptures. (Revelation 12:6, 14; compare Revelation 11:2, 3.) The seven literal years of Nebuchadnezzar's madness illustrated those "seven times" of 2,520 years, a year being represented by each day of a prophetic "time" of 360 days. (Ezekiel 4:6; Numbers 14:34) The symbolic "seven times" began when the armies of Babylon left Jerusalem and the

---

18. (a) During those Gentile Times the kingdom rule that should have been exercised by David's royal house was exercised by whom, and in what kind of way? (b) How was restoration of Messianic rule pictured?
19. (a) The Gentile Times numbering seven, what would be the length of each "time"? (b) About what time of the year did those Times begin, and about what time of year end?

land of Judah a desolation, with no governor to replace the murdered Governor Gedaliah in the land, about the middle of the lunar month of Tishri. So they would end about that time of the year in 1914 C.E., or about October 4/5, 1914.

20 At this latter time the reverse was to occur of what occurred in Tishri of 607 B.C.E., when the Gentile Times started. The land of Judah was left a desolate waste without a temple at Jerusalem, without "Jehovah's throne" there with an anointed descendant of King David seated thereon. (1 Chronicles 29:23) This meant that in early autumn of 1914 C.E. the trampling by the Gentile nations on the Messianic kingship was to cease and the Messianic kingdom was to be born, not at earthly Jerusalem, but up in heaven where the Son and Lord of King David now sat at the right hand of Jehovah God. (Psalm 110:1, 2) Then it was that the anointed one came "who has the legal right" and Jehovah God gave it to him.—Ezekiel 21:25-27; Daniel 7:13, 14.

21 World War I was already more than two months in progress when that marvelous event took place in the invisible heavens. In Revelation 12:1-5 that new-born Messianic kingdom is pictured as a male child to which God's heavenly "woman" gave birth and which was caught up to God's throne to share rulership with Him. So this majestic feature of God's "eternal purpose" triumphed, but against superhuman opposition. On this we read:

"And war broke out in heaven: Michael and his angels battled with the dragon, and the dragon and its angels battled but it did not prevail, neither was a place found for them any longer in heaven. So down the great dragon was hurled, the original serpent, the one called Devil and Satan, who is misleading the entire inhabited earth; he was hurled down to the earth, and his angels were hurled down with him. And I heard a loud voice in heaven say:

"'Now have come to pass the salvation and the power and the kingdom of our God and the authority of his Christ, because the accuser of our brothers has been hurled down, who accuses them day and night before our God! And they conquered him because of the blood of the Lamb and because of the word of their witnessing, and they did not love their souls even in the face of death. On this account be glad,

20. What would be meant when the reverse took place in 1914 C.E. of what occurred in 607 B.C.E.?
21. How was the birth of God's Messianic kingdom in heaven pictured, and what immediately followed?

you heavens and you who reside in them! Woe for the earth and for the sea, because the Devil has come down to you, having great anger, knowing he has a short period of time.'

"Now when the dragon saw that it was hurled down to the earth, it persecuted the woman that gave birth to the male child. . . . And the dragon grew wrathful at the woman, and went off to wage war with the remaining ones of her seed, who observe the commandments of God and have the work of bearing witness to Jesus."—Revelation 12:7-17.

²² Yes, the archangel Michael makes his appearance again in heaven, and, as the "seed" of God's "woman" who is destined to bruise the Serpent in the head, he wins the battle and hurls the original Serpent and his demon angels down to the earth. In his anger the Great Serpent persecutes the "woman" by persecuting the "remaining ones of her seed" who found themselves on earth during and since World War I. In his prophecy Jesus foretold such persecution of his anointed followers as due to occur during the "conclusion of the system of things." He said to his disciples:

"Then people will deliver you up to tribulation and will kill you, and you will be objects of hatred by all the nations on account of my name. . . . But he that has endured to the end is the one that will be saved."—Matthew 24:9-13.

²³ So the proof is at hand, from the Bible and from world history, that the "time of the end" began in early autumn of 1914. In full harmony with this fact, the persecution goes on of the anointed remnant, who "observe the commandments of God and have the work of bearing witness to Jesus." These are the ones who observe God's commandment given in Jesus' prophecy: "This good news of the kingdom will be preached in all the inhabited earth for a witness to all the nations." (Matthew 24:14) This remnant of anointed ones have identified themselves on the pages of history since 1914 C.E. Before this year members of this anointed remnant had been earnestly studying God's Word apart from Christendom. They put the Holy Bible ahead of man-made religious traditions. As early as 1876 they were publishing that the Gentile Times of 2,520 years would terminate in the year 1914. Events that have

22. (a) Michael's hurling of Satan and his demons out of heaven indicates what as to his identity? (b) How did Jesus foretell the persecutions that come upon the "remaining ones of [the woman's] seed"?
23. (a) The anointed remnant have identified themselves by obeying what command given through Jesus? (b) As early as when were they publishing the year for the Gentile Times to end?

taken place from that year onward prove they were not wrong.

²⁴ During World War I they became an object of hatred by all the nations and suffered severe persecution because they favored God's Messianic kingdom and tried to keep free from bloodguilt with which Christendom was staining herself. In 1919, the first postwar year, they discerned their Christian obligation to proclaim as never before God's Messianic kingdom, that had been set up in the heavens at the close of the Gentile Times in 1914. (Matthew 24:14) In the year 1925 their eyes of spiritual understanding were opened to see that the time had come for God to make a name for himself. (2 Samuel 7:23; Jeremiah 32:20; Isaiah 63:14; see *The Watch Tower* under date of August 1, 1925, page 226, column 2, paragraph 4; also September 15, 1925, page 280, paragraphs 41-43.) So now they bent themselves to the work of making known world wide the Bible name of the one living and true God and also His "eternal purpose that he formed in connection with the Christ, Jesus our Lord."—Ephesians 3:11.

²⁵ So in the year 1931, without presumptuousness but with full justification for the step now taken, they embraced a name that would distinguish them from Babylon the Great, the world empire of false religion, out of which they had come in obedience to God's command in Revelation 18:4. Yes, a name that would distinguish them even from Christendom with her hundreds of disunited sects and her worldliness and enormous bloodguilt. Indeed, a name that was based on Scripture (Isaiah 43:10, 12) and that would set their Christian work clearly before them. It was the name that has since become known world wide, a name both respected and hated, that is, Jehovah's witnesses. To this name they live up!

A "GREAT CROWD" TO SURVIVE HAR-MAGEDON

²⁶ Was all of this a mere short-lived burst of religious

---

24. (a) During World War I, why did the remnant become an object of international hatred? (b) What postwar work did they undertake, and what name did they seek to publicize?
25. From what did the anointed remnant need to distinguish themselves, and so what did they embrace in 1931 C.E.?
26. From how long ago has God been taking out a "people for his name," and is He lacking such a people today?

fervor? Was it a mere irrelevant accident? Or was this according to the progressive purpose of God? Look at the outcome! Something purposely started back there at Jerusalem on that historic day of Pentecost of 33 C.E. when God poured out his holy spirit and the spirit-filled apostle Peter stood up and quoted the prophecy of Joel 2:28-32 and said to thousands of Jews: "And everyone who calls on the name of Jehovah will be saved." There God began forming a "people for his name," a spiritual Israel. (Acts 2:1-21; 15:14) A further step was taken at the end of the 'seventieth week of years' in 36 C.E., when God sent the apostle Peter to preach to uncircumcised Gentiles and poured out his holy spirit upon these believing non-Jews. Thus God enlarged the "people for his name" by baptizing and anointing Gentiles with holy spirit and adding them to his spiritual Israel. (Acts 10:1 through 11:18; 15:7-11) That occurred back there in the first century. And what about today, in this twentieth century? The facts of unassailable history prove that God has succeeded in still having a "people for his name"!

[27] The presence today on earth of the final remnant of the spiritual "seed" of Abraham testifies that God is completing the full number of 144,000 spiritual Israelites under their Head, Jesus Christ. This despite all opposition from devils and men! His "eternal purpose that he formed in connection with the Christ" is triumphing—now! He is as unchangeably determined as ever to see his purpose through to its victorious realization in full in the near future. O what good this will mean for man! A "great crowd" of people who appreciate this fact is increasing world wide. Already they are receiving blessings through God's remnant of the spiritual "seed" of Abraham.

[28] The ancient patriarch Abraham pictured Jehovah God. Jehovah himself is the Greater Abraham. His "seed" is principally his once-sacrificed Son, Jesus Christ our Lord. Through his Principal One of the "seed" even all the members of spiritual Israel have been blessed. But does the blessing stop with them?

---

27. So what evidence have we today that God has stuck to his purpose in this regard, and blessings from this are now going to whom?
28. Who is principally the "seed" of Abraham, but what shows whether the blessing is limited to only those who are members of the "seed"?

No! God's sworn promise to ancient Abraham was: "By means of your seed all nations of the earth will certainly bless themselves." (Genesis 22:18; Acts 3:22-26) This "seed" includes more than Jesus Christ, for Abraham's seed was to be like the stars and the sands of the seashore—innumerable. Hence, the "seed" includes all spiritual Israel. By means of this entire "seed" others will procure a blessing, yes, "all nations of the earth" outside the "seed," outside spiritual Israel. So all mankind will be blessed by the "seed" of the Greater Abraham, Jehovah God, the heavenly Father of the spiritual "seed." With this end in view there will be a resurrection of the dead under the Messianic kingdom of the "seed."—Acts 24:15.

29 And who today of all nations are the ones who are receiving blessings through or in association with the "remnant" of the Abrahamic "seed"? According to God's loving purpose, these were foreshadowed in olden time. By whom?

30 When, back in 1513 B.C.E., the liberated Israelites left Egypt after the first Passover night and thereafter passed through the Red Sea to safety on the shores of the Sinaitic Peninsula, there was a "vast mixed company" of non-Israelites that went along with them. (Exodus 12:38; Numbers 11:4) When, in 607 B.C.E., the Babylonian armies destroyed Jerusalem for the first time, there were the Ethiopian eunuch, Ebed-melech, and the non-Israelite Rechabites who survived the destruction of the holy city and its temple. (Jeremiah 35:1-19; 38:7-12; 39:16-18) And, on Nisan 11 of 33 C.E., when Jesus foretold the destruction that was to come upon Jerusalem in the year 70 C.E. and that was a prophetic type of the destruction of Christendom in our generation, he said:

"Then there will be great tribulation such as has not occurred since the world's beginning until now, no, nor will occur again. In fact, unless those days were cut short, no flesh would be saved; but on account of the chosen ones those days will be cut short."—Matthew 24:21, 22; Mark 13:19, 20.

31 Besides the remnant of spiritual Israel, or "chosen

29, 30. (a) By whom were those now receiving blessings through the remnant of the "seed" foreshadowed in pre-Christian times? (b) How did Jesus refer to survivors of the coming "great tribulation"?
31. What vision was the apostle John given of the "great crowd" that survives the "tribulation" with the spiritual remnant?

ones," there will be survivors of that approaching "great tribulation." About the year 96 C.E., the aged apostle John was given a vision of these who go through the "great tribulation" in company with the "remnant" of spiritual Israel. Immediately after having a vision of the spiritual sealing of the 144,000 faithful members of spiritual Israel, John proceeds to say:

"After these things I saw, and, look! a great crowd, which no man was able to number, out of all nations and tribes and peoples and tongues, standing before the throne and before the Lamb, dressed in white robes; and there were palm branches in their hands. And they keep on crying with a loud voice, saying: 'Salvation we owe to our God, who is seated on the throne, and to the Lamb.'

"And in response one of the elders said to me: 'These who are dressed in the white robes, who are they and where did they come from?' So right away I said to him: 'My lord, you are the one that knows.' And he said to me: 'These are the ones that come out of the great tribulation, and they have washed their robes and made them white in the blood of the Lamb. That is why they are before the throne of God; and they are rendering him sacred service day and night in his temple; and the One seated on the throne will spread his tent over them. They will hunger no more nor thirst anymore, neither will the sun beat down upon them nor any scorching heat, because the Lamb, who is in the midst of the throne, will shepherd them, and will guide them to fountains of waters of life. And God will wipe out every tear from their eyes."—Revelation 7:9, 10, 13-17.

32 The explanation of the meaning of this vision that fits the facts of the day was published first in the year 1935 C.E., beginning with the Washington (D.C.) assembly of Jehovah's Christian witnesses on May 31, 1935. The "great crowd" seen in the vision do not expect to go to heaven and to reign on the heavenly Mount Zion with the 144,000 spiritual Israelites. For example, in Revelation 14:1-3 we read that the only ones that stand with the Lamb of God upon the heavenly Mount Zion are the 144,000 spiritual Israelites. The "great crowd" are not seen standing there, and for a good reason. Only of the 144,000 is it said: "These were bought from among mankind as firstfruits to God and to the Lamb." (Revelation 14:4, 5; James 1:18) Regarding the 144,000 who are "bought from among

32. (a) When was the explanation that fits the facts of our day first published regarding this vision? (b) Why is it to be expected that those of this "great crowd" will not go to heaven and reign with the Lamb of God?

mankind," we read these words addressed to the Lamb of God:

"You were slaughtered and with your blood you bought persons for God out of every tribe and tongue and people and nation, and you made them to be a kingdom and priests to our God, and they are to rule as kings over the earth."—Revelation 5:9, 10.

[33] So the purpose of God's "new covenant" with spiritual Israel is realized in those 144,000, because the new covenant was meant to produce a "kingdom of priests and a holy nation," a thing that the old Mosaic Law covenant did not produce. (Exodus 19:5, 6) The "great crowd" of Revelation 7:9-17 are not taken into that new covenant, but today they do associate with the "remnant" of spiritual Israelites who are in the new covenant.

[34] So the "great crowd" does not expect to go to heaven even after surviving the "great tribulation." Those of the "great crowd" expect the Lamb of God to shepherd them here on earth after the "great tribulation" and guide them to everlasting life in a Paradise earth. They acknowledge the enthroned God of heaven as the Universal Sovereign over all creation. They acknowledge the Messiah Jesus as "the Lamb of God that takes away the sin of the world" and admit that they owe their salvation to God through his once "slaughtered" Lamb and, by faith and obedience, "they have washed their robes and made them white in the blood of the Lamb."

[35] They acknowledge only the Sovereign Lord Jehovah as their God. This explains why they are seen "rendering him sacred service day and night in his temple," in the earthly courtyards of his spiritual temple, the Most Holy of which temple is in the holy heavens. (Hebrews 9:24) So the "great crowd" is now in contact with the remnant of the 144,000 spiritual Israelites who are prospective royal priests produced by the new covenant. In expression of their loyalty

33. In whom, then, is the purpose of God's new covenant realized?
34. Where do those of the "great crowd" expect to enjoy everlasting life, and what acknowledgment do they make of God and of his Lamb?
35. (a) Where in God's "temple" do they serve Him continually, and why? (b) How do they express loyalty to God's High Priest, and how did Jesus picture them in a parable?

to the royal High Priest Jesus Christ, those of the "great crowd" are loyal to his spiritual brothers who are yet on earth. They do all the good that they can to Christ's spiritual brothers, even joining them in preaching "this good news of the kingdom" world wide. These loyal ones are the "sheep" class whom Jesus described in his parable, saying:

"Then the king will say to those on his right, 'Come, you who have been blessed by my Father, inherit the kingdom prepared for you from the founding of the world. For I became hungry and you gave me something to eat; I got thirsty and you gave me something to drink. I was a stranger and you received me hospitably; naked, and you clothed me. I fell sick and you looked after me. I was in prison and you came to me.' Then the righteous ones will answer him with the words, 'Lord, when did we see you hungry and feed you, or thirsty, and give you something to drink? When did we see you a stranger and receive you hospitably, or naked, and clothe you? When did we see you sick or in prison and go to you?' And in reply the king will say to them, 'Truly I say to you, To the extent that you did it to one of the least of these my brothers, you did it to me.'

"And [the goat class] will depart into everlasting cutting-off, but the righteous ones into everlasting life."—Matthew 25:34-40, 46.

³⁶ Those who do not act like the "sheep" toward the spiritual brothers of the now reigning King Jesus Christ will be cut off in the oncoming "great tribulation," for they are not in favor of the "seed" of God's heavenly "woman" but are in favor of the "seed" of the "original serpent," Satan the Devil. (Genesis 3:15; Revelation 12:9, 17) They yield to the influence and guidance of the "original serpent, . . . who is misleading the entire inhabited earth," and so they will be found on the side of the "seed" of the Serpent when the "great tribulation" breaks out shortly.

³⁷ Since the birth of God's Messianic kingdom in the heavens in the year 1914, this worldly system of things has been in its "time of the end." This "time of the end" will soon culminate in the "great tribulation," as foretold by Jesus Christ. This unparalleled tribulation was foretold by the prophet Daniel long before Jehovah God sent his firstborn heavenly Son to earth to be called Jesus. Hence, God's angel worded the prophecy to Daniel in this way:

36. When will the goat class of the parable be 'cut off,' and why?
37. In what period is this worldly system now since 1914, and so what is this generation facing, according to Daniel 12:1?

"And during that time Michael will stand up, the great prince who is standing in behalf of the sons of your people. And there will certainly occur a time of distress such as has not been made to occur since there came to be a nation until that time."—Daniel 12:1; compare Matthew 24:21.

This generation of mankind is now facing that "time of distress."

38 During that "time of distress," that "great tribulation," antireligious political forces will destroy modern Babylon the Great, that is to say, the world empire of false religion that began with ancient Babylon. (Genesis 10:8-12; Revelation 17:1 through 18:24) Under God's protection members of the "remnant" of spiritual Israel and of the "great crowd" will survive that destruction as practicers of the true religion. (James 1:27) Immediately after that failure on the part of the antireligious forces to wipe out the clean and undefiled "form of worship," the pure religion, from the earth, there will come the "war of the great day of God the Almighty" at the place that is symbolically called Har–Magedon. (Revelation 16:14, 16) Why? Because the universal issue of Jehovah's creation-wide sovereignty, which the remnant and the "great crowd" uphold, must yet be settled. This settling of the issue is all part of God's "eternal purpose that he formed in connection with the Christ, Jesus our Lord," who is the principal one in God's promised "seed."

39 The national sovereignties, upon which political governments of today insist, clash with the Creator's Universal Sovereignty. The military confrontation over this paramount issue draws closer as this "time of the end" runs out. Do we, in the light of the Revelation's foreviews of coming events, see the earthly kings and political rulers and their armies and backers being gathered to the Har–Magedon battlefield for fighting it out to a finish? Yes.

40 However, we also see by faith the heavenly King of kings, Jesus Christ, and his angelic armies speeding to that same battlefield, as if riding on white war horses. We can take God's word for it; the war at

38. (a) What practicers of religion will survive destruction of Babylon the Great? (b) To settle what issue must the "war of the great day of God the Almighty" be fought?
39, 40. (a) Where will military confrontation over the issue take place, and whom do we see gathering there? (b) Who will prove to be superior there by victory?

Har–Magedon will culminate in victory for the forces of God the Almighty, and with destruction for all the man-made political systems and their officeholders, armies and patriotic supporters. The once Lamblike Jesus Christ will prove himself to be the King of kings, for Jehovah God will be at his right hand as a Fighter beside his King-Priest who is like Melchizedek.—Revelation 17:12-14; 19:11-21; Psalm 110:4, 5.

41 That is the grand climax of the "woe for the earth and for the sea" into which the "original serpent" and his demon angels, since their being ousted from heaven, lead all deceived mankind! (Revelation 12:7-12) With all his earthly "seed" destroyed at Har–Magedon, the "original serpent" will be unable to wage further war against the "remaining ones of [the woman's] seed" and the "great crowd" of fellow worshipers of the Sovereign Lord Jehovah. (Revelation 12:13, 17) Are the "original serpent" and his invisible demonic "seed" to be left on the loose in the vicinity of our earth down to which they have been ousted from heaven? No! For now comes the supreme moment for Jesus Christ the heavenly "seed" of God's "woman," who once was bruised at the heel by that murder-minded Serpent! The tables are turned, and now the "seed" of God's heavenly "woman" must bruise the Serpent "in the head," rendering him and his demonic "seed" as if they had not ever been! How?

42 By removing the Serpent and his demons from the neighborhood of the earth and hurling them into the "abyss" and sealing them up there, bound as with chains, for the next thousand years. Revelation 20:1-3 pictures this, not as a part of the war at Har–Magedon, but as a follow-up of that war. (Genesis 3:15; Romans 16:20; Luke 10:18-20) Thus the age-old Satanic "heavens" over earthly human society will be forever wiped out, and God's Messianic "new heavens" will spread themselves in blessing over the new earthly human society. O the triumphant realization then of the words of the apostle Peter, who, after describing the destruc-

---

41. (a) After Har–Magedon, why will the "original serpent" be unable to war further against the remnant and the "great crowd"? (b) In what sense will now come the supreme moment for the "seed" of God's "woman"?
42. (a) How, then, are the Serpent and his "seed" bruised? (b) What change then takes place as to heavenly ruling powers and earthly society?

tion of the old symbolic heavens and earth, encourages all true worshipers of Jehovah God by saying: "There are new heavens and a new earth that we are awaiting according to his promise, and in these righteousness is to dwell."—2 Peter 3:7-13; Revelation 20:11; 21:1; Isaiah 65:17.

CHAPTER 15

Making the Seventh Creative "Day" Sacred

FOR mankind's everlasting good, the long-awaited triumph of God's "eternal purpose that he formed in connection with the Christ, Jesus our Lord," is near at hand. Is this not something worth living for, something to see and benefit from with joy unspeakable? The surviving remnant of spiritual Israel and the "great crowd" of fellow witnesses of Jehovah will see such triumph and benefit from it to time eternal. But God's "eternal purpose" in connection with the "seed" of His heavenly "woman" will not then have come to its full accomplishment. It must carry on to further triumphs during and down to the end of the thousand years assigned for the reign of the Messiah Jesus and the 144,000 fellow members of "Abraham's seed." (Revelation 20:4-6; Galatians 3:8, 16, 29) How so?

2 Well, it was God's "eternal purpose" that mankind, who had been born into sin and death, should benefit by the bruising of the head of the Great Serpent. According to God's promise to Abraham, all families of the ground and all nations should bless themselves, procure an everlasting blessing, by means of the spiritual "seed" of Abraham. (Genesis 12:3; 22:18) The

1, 2. (a) With the bruising of the Great Serpent, will God's "eternal purpose" have reached its full accomplishment? (b) To whom was it God's purpose for the benefit from bruising the Serpent to come?

thousand years of Christ's reign will allow time for such work of blessing.

³ The Messiah Jesus and his glorified 144,000 associate kings and underpriests will have in mind the original purpose of God the Creator in putting man on earth in the Garden of Eden. That was to have all the earth to bloom as a global Garden of Eden. It was God's original unalterable purpose to have all this Paradise earth filled with perfect righteous men and women, these to live here forever and ever in peaceful loving relationship with the heavenly Father as members of his universal family of heaven and earth, members of His universal organization. All the fish of the sea and the flying creatures of the heavens and all living moving creatures on the earth, domestic and wild, would be in safe, harmless subjection to this godly human race. (Genesis 1:26-31; Isaiah 45:18; Psalm 115:16; 104:5) For the realization of this, God's original purpose, the "seed" of God's heavenly "woman" must reign for the thousand years. The work of accomplishing this was assigned to the Messiah Jesus, who, when on earth, was called "the Son of man." —Psalm 8:4-8; Hebrews 2:5-9.

⁴ Consequently, after the surviving remnant of spiritual Israel finish their course on earth and are glorified with the reigning Messiah Jesus and all his other joint heirs, the "great crowd" of other "tribulation" survivors will not be left alone on the cleansed earth. They are too few to "fill the earth." Furthermore, they were not the only ones ransomed by the perfect human sacrifice of the Lord Jesus Christ; he was bruised "in the heel" in order to "taste death for every man"; he "gave himself a corresponding ransom for all." (Hebrews 2:9; 1 Timothy 2:5, 6) The vast majority of those ransomed ones are now dead in the common grave of mankind. How will they be enabled to benefit from Messiah's ransom? By the promised resurrection of the dead. (Job 14:13, 14; Isaiah 26:19; Matthew 22:31, 32; John 5:28, 29; Acts 24:15; Revelation 20: 12-14) Thus the surviving "great crowd" will be joined

---

3. For the realization of what original purpose of God must there be a thousand-year reign over earth, and by whom?
4. Why, after glorification of the remnant of spiritual Israel, will the surviving "great crowd" not be left to be the only human occupants of the earth?

by those billions of resurrected ones, all of them being the descendants of that original human pair, Adam and Eve. What a global family reunion!

5 There is now a special purpose that the reigning Jesus Christ and his 144,000 joint heirs must carry out. What is this? The making of God's seventh creative "day" a blessed day, a sacred day. After God created Adam and Eve and gave them their commission of work, setting before them their purpose in life in Paradise, the sixth creative "day" of God ended and the seventh creative "day" began, about six thousand years ago. He ordained this creative "day" as a Sabbath "day" for Himself. On it he would desist from earthly creative work, resting from such work, not because of weariness, but to let the first human pair and their descendants worship Him as their only living and true God by serving him, carrying out the service that he had assigned to them. He knew that his stated purpose for them could be carried out during the next seven-thousand-year period, His Sabbath "day."

"God proceeded to bless the seventh day and make it sacred, because on it he has been resting from all his work that God has created for the purpose of making."—Genesis 2:3.

6 Very soon thereafter the spirit son of God that made himself Satan the Devil proceeded to desecrate that holy seventh creative "day" of Jehovah God. For six thousand years he and his "seed" have been allowed to continue their effort to make it seem to be a cursed "day," unsacred, disturbing to God's "rest," to try to make him violate his own ordained Sabbath "day." But in vain! During the thousand years that the Great Serpent and his demon "seed" are abyssed, Jehovah God will reverse all the wickedness that such desecraters of Jehovah's Sabbath have done in the earth. By means of the thousand-year reign of his Son Jesus Christ, Jehovah God will uplift the human race, which descended from the original human pair, back to human perfection and sinlessness, only the rebellious, disobedient ones of the race being destroyed as having no respect for the great Sabbath "day" of Jehovah God.

5. (a) What other purpose of God was there for Christ and his 144,000 to carry out? (b) How did God proceed to rest on his seventh creative "day"?
6. (a) How has God's seventh creative "day" been desecrated as His Sabbath day? (b) Nevertheless, how will God make it a blessed, sacred "day"?

(Revelation 20:14, 15) Paradise will be restored to earth and made earth wide. The whole earth will be filled with humankind from the first human pair, all the earth being then subdued.—Genesis 1:28.

⁷ By the fulfillment of God's "eternal purpose that he formed in connection with the Christ, Jesus our Lord," God's seventh creative "day" will end up blessed, sacred, sanctified. Jehovah's having blessed that "day" six thousand years ago and his then making it sacred will not have been counteracted to His eternal reproach. The Messianic prayer, "Let your kingdom come. Let your will take place, as in heaven, also upon earth," will stand gloriously fulfilled. (Matthew 6:10) Having served Jehovah's "eternal purpose" to a God-honoring triumph of that purpose, Jesus Christ then "hands over the kingdom to his God and Father," thus subjecting himself to the Universal Sovereign, Jehovah Most High. (1 Corinthians 15:24-28) Loyally he vindicates Jehovah's universal sovereignty.

JUSTIFICATION OF OBEDIENT MANKIND TO ETERNAL LIFE

⁸ Restored mankind are now on their own, just as the innocent perfect Adam and Eve were in the paradisaic Garden of Eden when God gave them their assignment of sacred service to Him. Who among restored mankind in the Paradise earth will remain loyal to the universal sovereignty and Godship of the loving Creator, Jehovah the Source of all life? Whom will he himself justify or declare righteous to everlasting life on the Paradise earth? To test all restored mankind on this vital score, Jehovah accepts the kingdom handed over by Jesus Christ and has the Great Serpent and his demons released from their abyss. He lets these unreformed spirit rebels try to tempt and mislead mankind again.

⁹ Jehovah does not deny that some of restored mankind will let themselves be misled by Satan and his demons, just as the perfect Adam and Eve in the

---

7. What prayer taught by Jesus will thus be fulfilled, and how will he then show recognition of Jehovah's universal sovereignty?
8. Restored mankind will then be on what standing before God, and before justifying any to eternal life, what will He do?
9. (a) What befalls the restored humans who yield to deception by the Serpent and his demons? (b) How is the final stage of God's "eternal purpose" carried out?

Garden of Eden did. He allows for an unnumbered crowd to do so. When the test has been permitted to the full extent and has unalterably divided mankind as to how individuals stand as regards universal sovereignty and Godship, destruction comes from heaven upon the human rebels. Finally, the turn comes for the great desecrater of Jehovah's Sabbath, Satan the Devil, and his demon "seed" to be destroyed. Doubtless this will be done by means of the "seed" of God's heavenly "woman," for that "seed" was assigned to bruise the Serpent "in the head," according to God's "eternal purpose" as stated in the Garden of Eden. (Genesis 3:15) No return to the abyss for Satan the Devil and his demons, but utter destruction as by fire mingled with sulphur will be their portion. There will be no temporary recovery from this final stage of the crushing of the Great Serpent's head. No further opportunities for him to act as a Tempter are allowed for. —Revelation 20:7-10.

10 What a crowning triumph that will be for God's "eternal purpose that he formed in connection with the Christ, Jesus our Lord"! Those of restored mankind who demonstrate their unchangeable determination to serve and obey Jehovah as the Universal Sovereign and the one living and true God, He will declare righteous. Upon these justified ones he will bestow the gift reward of everlasting life in the everblooming earthly Paradise, God's footstool. (Isaiah 66:1) He will fill their endless lives with ever-satisfying, ever-stimulating purpose, to His glory by His Christ, Jesus our Lord. (Revelation 21:1-5) Hallelujah!—Psalm 150:6.

11 Here is a prospect for mankind without compare! It is for those who now harmonize their lives with God's "eternal purpose." Nothing finer could there be than to make God's purpose our purpose.

---

10. How will those proving loyal to Jehovah's sovereignty and Godship be rewarded?
11. What fine thing is there for us to do with regard to that incomparable purpose of God?

GOD'S PURPOSE FURTHER CLARIFIED

To learn more about God's eternal purpose, obtain and read—

✔ **God's Kingdom of a Thousand Years Has Approached:** This 416-page volume gives you thrilling details about the thousand-year reign of Jesus Christ. It also explains his prophetic parables of the ten virgins, the talents and the sheep and goats. Send just 50c.

✔ **Is This Life All There Is?:** Here is a pocket-size book of 192 pages that presents the revealing truth about life after death. It shows you the way to a successful life now as well as a secure and abiding future in God's new order. Just send 25c for this book, or 75c for both of these books. Write to **Watchtower** at an address given below.

ALASKA 99507: 2552 East 48th Ave., Anchorage. AUSTRALIA: 11 Beresford Road, Strathfield, N.S.W. 2135. BAHAMAS: Box N-1247, Nassau, N.P. BARBADOS, W.I.: Fontabelle Rd., Bridgetown. BELIZE: Box 257, Belize City. BRAZIL: Rue Guaíra, 216, Bosque da Saúde, 04142 São Paulo, SP. CANADA: 150 Bridgeland Ave., Toronto, Ont. M6A 1Z5. CONGO REPUBLIC: B.P. 2.114, Brazzaville. ENGLAND: Watch Tower House, The Ridgeway, London NW7 1RN. FIJI: Box 23, Suva. FRANCE: 81 rue du Point-du-Jour, 92100 Boulogne-Billancourt. GERMANY (WESTERN): Postfach 13025, 62 Wiesbaden-Dotzheim. GHANA: Box 760, Accra. GUYANA: 50 Brickdam, Georgetown 16. HAWAII 96814: 1228 Pensacola St., Honolulu. HONG KONG: 312 Prince Edward Rd., Second Floor, Kowloon. INDIA: South Avenue, Santa Cruz, Bombay 400054. INDONESIA: Jl Batuceper 47, Jakarta Pusat, DKI. IRELAND: 86 Lindsay Rd., Glasnevin, Dublin 9. JAMAICA, W.I.: 41 Trafalgar Rd., Kingston 10. KENYA: Box 47788, Nairobi. LEEWARD ISLANDS, W.I.: Box 119, St. Johns, Antigua. LIBERIA: P.O. Box 171, Monrovia. MALAYSIA: 20 Scotland Close, Penang. NEWFOUNDLAND, CANADA A1C 2M1: 239 Pennywell Rd., St. John's. NEW ZEALAND: 6-A Western Springs Rd., Auckland 3. NIGERIA: P.O. Box 194, Yaba, Lagos State. PAKISTAN: 8-E Habibullah Rd., Lahore 3. PANAMA: Apartado 1386, Panama 1. PAPUA NEW GUINEA: Box 113, Port Moresby. PHILIPPINE REPUBLIC: 186 Roosevelt Ave., San Francisco del Monte, Quezon City D-503. RHODESIA: P.O. Box 1462, Salisbury. SIERRA LEONE: Box 136, Freetown. SOUTH AFRICA: Private Bag 2, P.O. Elandsfontein 1406. SRI LANKA, REP. OF: 62 Layard's Road, Colombo 5. SWITZERLAND: Ulmenweg 45, P.O. Box 477, CH-3601 Thun. TRINIDAD, W.I.: 2 La Seiva Road, Maraval, Port of Spain. UNITED STATES OF AMERICA: 117 Adams St., Brooklyn, N.Y. 11201.